MUCH TO LEARN, MUCH TO GIVE

Ellen Lawrence, circa 1915. BIA personnel files, NARA (St. Louis).

MUCH TO LEARN, MUCH TO GIVE

Ellen Lawrence, Teacher of Pueblo Textile Arts

Leslie Perrin Wilson

© 2025 by Leslie Perrin Wilson
All Rights Reserved
No part of this book may be reproduced in any form or by any electronic or mechanical means including information storage and retrieval systems without permission in writing from the publisher, except by a reviewer who may quote brief passages in a review.

Sunstone books may be purchased for educational, business, or sales promotional use. For information please write: Special Markets Department, Sunstone Press, P.O. Box 2321, Santa Fe, New Mexico 87504-2321.
Printed on acid-free paper
∞

LIBRARY OF CONGRESS CATALOGING IN PUBLICATION DATA

(ON FILE)

WWW.SUNSTONEPRESS.COM
SUNSTONE PRESS / POST OFFICE BOX 2321 / SANTA FE, NM 87504-2321 /USA
(505) 988-4418

For Anni, Lil, and Dale

Contents

List of Illustrations ~ 9

Introduction ~ 11

1 / Beginnings ~ 25

2 / Farm Wife ~ 37

3 / Lace Teacher ~ 51

4 / Field Matron ~ 77

5 / Beyond Assimilation ~ 109

6 / Albuquerque Indian School—A Bumpy Start ~ 123

7 / Teacher of Pueblo Textile Arts ~ 137

8 / After the BIA ~ 157

Postscript ~ 163

Acknowledgments ~ 165

Sources ~ 167

Index ~ 196

List of Illustrations

1. Ellen Lawrence, circa 1915. BIA personnel files, NARA (St. Louis).

2. First page of Ellen Lawrence's letter to niece Mildred Ross, Jemez, New Mexico, July 10, 1922. Photographed from original in author's collection.

3. Hopi man weaving a sash for a ceremonial kilt on a narrow upright loom, Arizona, circa 1898. University of Southern California collections. Reproduced by permission.

4. Ellen Lawrence with California lace-making Indians. *Sunset, the Pacific Monthly* (May 1919).

5. Pueblo of Jemez from the east, circa 1925. Elsie Clews Parsons, *The Pueblo of Jemez* (1925). Reproduced courtesy of Boston Athenaeum.

6. Pueblo of Jemez, plaza, circa 1925. Elsie Clews Parsons, *The Pueblo of Jemez* (1925). Reproduced courtesy of Boston Athenaeum.

7. Charles Lummis, photographer. Pueblo woman weaving belt on a belt loom, 1889. Library of Congress collections.

8. San Felipe Pueblo, between 1871 and 1907. NARA (College Park).

9. 3 Hawks, photographer. Aerial view of Albuquerque Indian School, 1932. Albuquerque Museum (transfer from Albuquerque Public Library). Reproduced by permission.

10. Ellen Lawrence standing by loom at Albuquerque Indian School. *The Pow-Wow, 1931. The Fifth Annual* (Albuquerque Indian School, 1931).

11. Ellen Lawrence wearing manta of cloth she wove and embroidered. *Albuquerque Tribune* (May 30, 1936).

Introduction

In July 1922, Ellen Lawrence—a Bureau of Indian Affairs field matron in Jemez, New Mexico—wrote her nineteen-year-old niece Mildren Ross, urging the young woman to travel from Texas for a visit. Lawrence, who had been posted at the Pueblo of Jemez in 1919, was now moving into larger rented quarters: "For a week I have been cleaning an old mud house up and moving into it. I am not done yet but I can see the end of the job."[1] Her new home, she wrote Mildred, was the old Presbyterian mission. For the first time at Jemez, she had sufficient space to accommodate a guest: "The three little rooms I had was not nearly enough. I am now occupying six rooms of a seven-room house. There is plenty of room for you and I do hope you come to see us soon."

> Jemez, New Mex
> July 10, 1922
>
> My dear Mildred
>
> You had my post office all right but I did not write at once as I was too rushed with work. For a week I have been cleaning an old mud house up and moving into it. I am not done yet but I can see the end of the job.
>
> I wanted to get into a larger house for several reasons.

First page of Ellen Lawrence's letter to niece Mildred Ross, Jemez, New Mexico, July 10, 1922. Photographed from original in author's collection.

Located in Sandoval County, in the Cañon de San Diego on the east bank of the Jemez River, surrounded by cliffs and mountains, Jemez is starkly beautiful, its rugged landscape enhanced on a bright day by the intense contrast of sun-drenched red clay soil and turquoise sky. It is also remote—fifty-plus miles from Albuquerque, from which it was accessible in 1922 by a stage that made a single round trip daily to Jemez Springs, a popular resort area about twelve miles north of Jemez. Ellen Lawrence informed her niece, "You have to pass right by my door to go from Albuquerque to Jemez Springs." For those traveling by automobile, transportation had improved with the construction a few years before of a "fairly good road from Albuquerque—at least it is passable for autos." As Ellen noted, hired cars also regularly carried passengers between Albuquerque and Jemez Springs. Regardless of the conveyance used, the trip from Albuquerque to Jemez would have required Mildred to spend a night in an Albuquerque hotel and a good part of another day in transportation on top of the more than seven hundred miles already traveled from San Antonio.

The Pueblo of Jemez—historically the village of Walatowa—is home to descendants of a once numerous and powerful people who relocated from the Four Corners region in the thirteenth century and who, in the 1830s, took in the surviving population of the Pecos Pueblo, which had been diminished by disease and the predations of other tribes. (Towa, the language of the inhabitants of both Jemez and Pecos, formed a natural bond.) The ancestors of the Jemez people had occupied many structures over an extended geographical area. But their number and dominion waned dramatically after the arrival of the Spanish in the mid-sixteenth century.[2]

In the 1920s, the federally administered Pueblo of Jemez was sparsely inhabited (population 561 in 1921[3]). It also remained largely incommunicado with the outside world. In a 1925 inspection report, Elinor D. Gregg (Supervisor of Field Nurses and Field Matrons with the BIA) observed that Jemez was one of only two pueblos within the Southern Pueblos Agency without telephone service.[4] The doctor for emergency medical situations had to be contacted by mail, which hardly worked in favor of saving lives. Leo Crane, Superintendent of the Southern Pueblos Agency, wrote in his February 1, 1921 evaluation of Lawrence of the "isolation of this pueblo" and of the "little advanced and re-actionary condition of the people," and commented that the poor quarters there worked against "the keeping of highly-efficient employees."[5]

Ellen Lawrence had some appreciation of the history of her location. She was aware that New Mexico had been "settled by white people long before

Jamestown and Plymouth" and she was interested in archeological activity in the vicinity of the Pueblo of Jemez. She wrote Mildred that they might visit the "excavations at the old-old mission that has been buried so long and they are now digging out."[6] She was nevertheless conscious of the disadvantages of Jemez. "This is the deadest place you ever dreamed of," she wrote, adding "I try to imagine what it was like 300 years ago. 'They say' that it was even less civilized then than it is now—but that seems impossible."

Yet she was unfazed by the challenges that life in Jemez presented. In fact, her six-year employment there (1919–1925) proved to be a turning point for her. The place provided opportunity for growth and self-realization through the acquisition of skills that would later define her. This middle-aged Anglo woman had the grit to make the situation work for her. She was resourceful, self-reliant, and receptive to the culture around her. She possessed a drive to express herself in ways that reflected who she was and, at the same time, was able to maximize on the limited possibilities for self-expression within the BIA hierarchy. But it was not easy for her.

Ellen Lawrence was no line-toeing government bureaucrat. Although she was generally evaluated as a solid and dependable employee, one supervisor commented pointedly on "the form and brevity of her regular weekly reports which are not indicative of interest or enthusiasm."[7] Another (Reuben Perry of the Albuquerque Indian School) found her difficult to understand and manage, even quirky. She was direct and resilient, adaptive without being acquiescent. But nothing stood out markedly in her personal profile to indicate that she might ultimately harness the federal system to her advantage.

Her BIA personnel files reveal that Ellen Lawrence was fifty-one years old in 1922, five feet four and a half inches tall, and weighed in the vicinity of one hundred and twenty-five pounds. She wore eyeglasses. A Presbyterian of Scots-Irish descent, she was married to a considerably older man and had one child (a son). Her husband lived with her in Jemez; their son was grown and on his own.

Born Mary Ellen Ross in Missouri in 1871, she moved as a girl with her family to Texas. Educated through three years of high school, she taught school until she married and became a farm wife and mother. From an early age, she was—like many other women of her time—a skilled needleworker and craftswoman. Eventually, in support of her family, she transformed her facility with traditional women's occupations from avocation to vocation, transcending conventional expectations for a married woman of her time. She formally entered the Indian Service in 1915 as a teacher of lace making to Native Americans in southern California and was transferred to Jemez in 1919 as a field matron. She became familiar with Pueblo crafts and culture in New Mexico, where she worked at Jemez, San Felipe, and Albuquerque until 1936, learning Native weaving and embroidery while living among the Pueblos.

Over more than two decades, service in the Bureau of Indian Affairs reinforced Ellen Lawrence's consciousness of her particular capabilities and fueled her desire to exercise and share them. She came into her own during the early to mid-1930s, a period when authentic Native design and technique were promoted through the Laboratory of Anthropology in Santa Fe and during which she taught Native handicrafts at the Albuquerque Indian School. She strove to pursue her personal interests as she forged a meaningful connection with the indigenous people with whom she worked—both in some ways despite her position in the flawed federal Indian school system.

Ellen Lawrence was not driven by a particular commitment to the BIA agenda in entering the Indian Service in 1915. Nor did she regard Native Americans through a romantic or sentimental lens. In her 1922 letter, she urged her niece to get to Jemez by August 2 for the Fiesta of Persingula (patron saint of the Jemez Pueblo), a blended Catholic and Native festival open to visitors, featuring the traditional corn dance and the Pecos bull.[8] Her subsequent comments suggest a more matter-of-fact than idealized regard for the celebration, which she described as "worth seeing—once," adding, "Try to get here at least a week before the dance so you will get used to the Indians and not be scared to death when you see them dancing with almost no clothes on!" She began working for the BIA in 1915 because she needed to support herself and her husband and along the way developed fellow feeling for the people she came to know through her employment.

Nor was she one of the cadre of relatively privileged New Mexico arts and crafts devotees drawn to Indian handicraft by an embrace of aesthetics or an inclination toward cultural relativism. She had moved from California to Jemez primarily for pragmatic reasons. In this she differed from the many creative people—among them artist Georgia O'Keefe and writer Willa Cather—who sought inspiration in New Mexico roughly simultaneously with Lawrence's early years there.

All of this made her something of an unlikely champion of Pueblo textile arts, an outlier in a relatively more empowered field of advocates. Nevertheless, she effectively participated in elevating the status of these Native crafts at a moment of growing interest in them at the national, regional, and local levels.

Ellen Lawrence's enthusiasm for Native textile crafts coincided with a remodeling of BIA objectives between her entry into the Indian Service and her retirement in 1936. In the late nineteenth century, the goal was to assimilate Native children into American culture by eradicating Indian identity and inculcating white, Christian values and ways in government-operated Indian schools.[9] This equated to the suppression of Native language, customs, and religion and the elevation of national at the expense of tribal identity. Bureau administrators like Estelle Reel (Superintendent of Indian Schools from 1898 to 1910) approached the handcrafting of Native products as relevant primarily to the degree that it contributed to economic self-sufficiency, and to regard fidelity to traditional designs and techniques as important mainly in relation to satisfying market demand for authenticity.[10] Those at the top of the bureaucratic pyramid might pay lip service to the inherent worth of Native culture—BIA Commissioner Francis Leupp wrote in his 1905 *Report of the Commissioner of Indian Affairs*, "Let us not make the mistake, in the process of absorbing them, of washing out of them whatever is distinctly Indian"[11]—but took few steps to safeguard it.

Over time, the BIA acknowledged that assimilation and the perpetuation of Native practices might not be incompatible. Artists, arts and crafts enthusiasts, anthropologists, social scientists, and others who found intrinsic merit in Indian culture protested government disregard for it and pressed for reform. A movement to protect Native Americans from abuses of their lands, heritage, and rights led to changes in Indian school curricula and focused renewed attention on Native handicrafts. The New Mexico Association on Indian Affairs was founded in 1922, the American Indian Defense Association in 1923, and the Indian Arts Fund in Santa Fe by Kenneth Chapman in the same year. In 1928, the seminal document *The Problem of Indian Administration* (the Meriam Report) was issued by the Institute for Government Research to identify and address problems created by adherence to government policy. During the 1930s, with the election of Franklin Delano Roosevelt to the presidency, the appointment of John Collier as Commissioner of Indian Affairs, and Collier's advocacy of the Indian Reorganization Act of 1934 and the Indian Arts and Crafts Act of 1935, Native handicrafts resurged.[12] In this supportive climate, an Indian arts and crafts program at the Santa Fe Indian School was established (1932) and, simultaneously, Ellen Lawrence attained respect and recognition as an accomplished practitioner and teacher of Pueblo textile arts at the Albuquerque Indian School.

Lawrence took enormous satisfaction from her work among the Pueblos, which allowed her to channel an impulse manifested early in life to master and practice handiwork in various forms and to transmit her expertise to others. Unremarkable though she was in most respects, she was drawn to handiwork that required a high degree of precision and skill and that approached and sometimes crossed the indistinct boundary between craft and art. She made the most of her opportunities, transforming work that her own culture deemed appropriate for her sex into a sustained career at a time when American women represented little more than twenty percent of the workforce.[13] On one level, she reflected the proclivity of working women early in the twentieth century to prefer jobs that reinforced the definition of their role as workers in terms of "values appropriate to...home life."[14] But she did not simply accept the boundaries of the positions she filled—she actively incorporated handiwork—the work she wanted to do—into assignments in which it was not an explicit duty.

The history of the Pueblo textile arts that Ellen Lawrence took up at Jemez reaches back over two millennia.¹⁵ The Ancestral Puebloan people of the Rio Grande wove fabric from plant and animal fibers using finger techniques. Later, the backstrap (or belt) loom was introduced, and cotton fiber was acquired from other Southwestern tribes. The upright loom, attached to a ceiling or beam above, was in regular use by 1000 A.D., and Rio Grande Pueblos eventually grew their own cotton. When the Spanish entered the Southwest in the sixteenth century, they observed that the Native people were garbed in well-made cotton clothing. The Spanish brought churro sheep with them, and the Pueblos began to use wool as well as cotton for weaving cloth; merino wool replaced churro in the late nineteenth century.

Hopi man weaving a sash for a ceremonial kilt on a narrow upright loom, Arizona, circa 1898. University of Southern California collections. Reproduced by permission.

Unlike the Navajos, who learned to weave from the Pueblos and eventually supplied them with cloth and blankets superior to those they (the Pueblos) had been making, the Rio Grande Pueblos of New Mexico traditionally wove mainly for internal use or for gift rather than for commercial trade. (Under compulsion, they also provided the Spanish with fabric.) They wove both ceremonial garments and clothing for daily use—mantas, dresses, dance kilts, breech cloths, shirts, shawls, belts, and sashes—and made some items—hair ties, garters, and leggings—by various other fiber techniques. Pueblo woven products were subtle in color and design, but could be enlivened by a range of decorative techniques, including dying, painting, brocading, and embroidery. From the late nineteenth century, as commercially woven fabric took the place of hand-woven, the Pueblos applied embroidery to decorate items made from it, as well.

Spanish authority and culture held sway in New Mexico from 1540 to 1848, when the war between the United States and Mexico ended with the Treaty of Guadalupe Hidalgo. For over three hundred years, the Spanish had influenced the forms, designs, and raw material of Native textiles, and may also have introduced embroidery. But there was relatively little change over this period in the technology and techniques of Pueblo textile production or in the types of clothing required for ritual purposes. Pueblo textiles entered a new era under American control, labeled by specialists the "classic" period, which continued to about 1880, by which date the railroads had arrived in New Mexico. At the beginning of the classic period, the key characteristics of Rio Grande Pueblo textiles had been well-established. As it concluded, the influx of bright modern dyes, machine-made yarns, cotton string, and, ultimately, trade cloth and commercially made clothing had started to alter the practice of Pueblo embroidery and to dwindle the need for hand weaving.[16]

The weaving and embroidery designs that had prevailed before the annexation of Southwestern territory by the United States continued in use throughout the classic period and became prototypical in local and broader consciousness of traditional Pueblo textile craft. As anthropologist Kate Peck Kent has written, surviving specimens from this this period "make up the nucleus of our fine old museum collections and define traditional

Pueblo weaving for people today."[17] The Pueblo embroidery designs and techniques that Ellen Lawrence learned at Jemez in the 1920s almost certainly reflected those prevalent during the three decades of the classic period.

Traditional Pueblo embroidery in the Rio Grande villages was as vibrant as traditional Pueblo weaving was subtle.[18] It was the dominant decorative technique through the period of heavy Spanish influence and the classic period, as well. It featured bold-colored wool yarn worked in the Pueblo stitch—a variety of back-stitch unique to the Pueblos, useful for efficiently and economically filling in large areas of fabric—and other more commonplace embroidery stitches. Pueblo embroidery designs from prehistoric (that is, pre-Spanish) times were employed through the classic period and, due in part to their reproduction in H. P. Mera's *Pueblo Indian Embroidery* in 1943, continue in use today. Those interested in Pueblo embroidery have disagreed about whether early designs were symbolic and stylized or simply abstract, and, if symbolic, what they actually represented. Regardless, their endurance speaks to the power of their authenticity and cultural significance to the Native people who have perpetuated them.

Embroidery was a specialty of the Zuni, Acoma, Santa Clara, and Jemez Pueblos, in particular. In the nineteenth century, Jemez became known for embroidered shirts and, later, embroidered vests. Ellen Lawrence's transfer to Jemez in 1919 was a fortuitous placement.

For most of its history, Pueblo weaving was primarily a man's occupation, while embroidery was, at least in some New Mexico pueblos, mainly woman's work. In the late nineteenth and early twentieth centuries, Pueblo men increasingly transitioned into America's wage economy, which kept them away from the pueblo and reduced the amount of time available for weaving, ultimately resulting in the near-abandonment of the craft. Women took a greater role in weaving only with revival efforts in the twentieth century. Weaving as it had long been practiced at most of the New Mexico pueblos had largely ceased by the time Ellen Lawrence went to Jemez as a field matron.

Lawrence's capability and persistence earned her the respect of both the Pueblos and of knowledgeable and influential New Mexico Anglos—Kenneth Chapman included—devoted to preserving and promoting Native arts and crafts. And through her work, she tapped into shared values that crossed the line between cultures. In doing so, she lastingly enhanced some Native lives.

There is ample documentation of Ellen Lawrence's working life under the BIA, but it is of a kind that requires some reading between the lines. BIA records constitute official public record—they were not created to capture personal thoughts and feelings. Ellen's voice is subdued in the files kept on her for more than twenty years. She expresses in administrative paperwork only what an employee would consider appropriate to express to an employer. If papers of a more personal nature or specimens of her Pueblo handiwork survive, they have not materialized. Despite this, it is possible to trace the trajectory of her career.

Moreover, other sources exist to confirm the impact of Ellen Lawrence's work on Pueblos who were receptive to what she had to teach, foremost among them award-winning Jemez Pueblo artist Lucy Yepa Lowden (1916–2005). Lowden was a child at Jemez when Lawrence worked there and was later one of Lawrence's students, her assistant, and her successor at the Albuquerque Indian School. In several interviews given for newspaper articles, Lowden abundantly credited Lawrence's influence on her path in life. She also wrote a well-known poem addressed to her non-Indian friends, which appears on a display wall inside the heritage center at the Jemez Historic Site. That poem includes the lines "You are also great people / with much to learn, / much to give."[19] This recognition of a dynamic of positive Native/Anglo exchange might well have been directed to the memory of Ellen Lawrence, among other friends. Over the course of her working life in New Mexico, Ellen Lawrence practiced a reciprocity—a sharing of mutually valued skills—with the Pueblos among whom she worked. Her attraction to Pueblo textile handicrafts sprang from an understanding of what mattered to her, a reliance on person-to-person connection, and an elemental cultural appreciation. Hers was not a simple tale of cultural appropriation. In its greater complexity, her story is worth telling.

NOTES

1. Ellen Lawrence, autograph letter, signed, Jemes (Jemez), New Mexico, July 10, 1922, to Mildred Ross (San Antonio, Texas), author's collection.

2. Joe S. Sando, *Nee Hemish: A History of Jemez Pueblo* (Santa Fe: Clear Light Publishing, 2008); Daniel Gibson, *Pueblos of the Rio Grande: A Visitor's Guide* (Tucson: Rio Nuevo Publishers, 2011), 33, 35; Ana Pacheco, *Pueblos of New Mexico* (Charleston, South Carolina: Arcadia Publishing, 2018), 61.

3. United States, Department of the Interior, Bureau of Indian Affairs, personnel records for Ellen Lawrence, 1909-1936 *(henceforth cited as BIA personnel records)*, Superintendent Leo Crane, Southern Pueblos Agency (Albuquerque, New Mexico), efficiency report, June 30, 1921, National Archives, St. Louis.

4. United States, Department of the Interior, Bureau of Indian Affairs, central classified files, 1907-1939, Elinor D. Gregg, "Report on Health Activities, Southern Pueblos. Visited April 26th to May 7th, 1925," 4, National Archives, Washington, DC *(henceforth cited as Gregg, "Report")*. *Regarding the use of "BIA":* Throughout the narrative of this book, although not necessarily in all footnotes and source listings, the acronym "BIA" is used to refer to the governmental department known variously as the Office of Indian Affairs, the Bureau of Indian Affairs, the Indian Office, and the Indian Service.

5. BIA personnel records, Superintendent Leo Crane, Southern Pueblos Agency (Albuquerque, New Mexico), efficiency report, Feb. 1, 1921, National Archives, St. Louis.

6. The seventeenth-century mission church San José de los Jémez, which was under excavation in 1921 and 1922.

7. BIA personnel records, Special Supervisor in Charge Chester E. Faris, Southern Pueblos Agency (Albuquerque, New Mexico), typed letter, signed, June 23, 1924, to "The Commissioner of Indian Affairs" [Charles Henry Burke] (Washington, DC).

8. Sando, *Nee Hemish*, 212-213.

9. "The preparation of Indian youth for the duties, privileges, and

responsibilities of American citizenship is the purpose of the governmental plan of education. This implies training in the industrial arts, the development of the moral and intellectual faculties, the establishment of good habits, the formation of character, and preparation for citizenship... These [Indian] schools should be conducted upon lines best adapted to the development of character, and the formation of habits of industrial thrift and moral responsibility, which will prepare the pupil for the active responsibilities of citizenship."—United States, Department of the Interior, Office of Indian Affairs, *Rules, Indian School Service* (Washington: Government Printing Office, 1898), 3.

10. In her 1901 *Course of Study for the Indian Schools of the United States*, Reel wrote, "Indian work is always in demand, but is difficult to obtain, since the tendency of the tribes is to copy from modern wares, and the work is not distinctively Indian. A good living is in the hands of those who will faithfully portray the work of their ancestors."—United States, Department of the Interior, Office of Indian Affairs, *Course of Study for the Indian Schools of the United States. Industrial and Literary* (Washington: Government Printing Office, 1901), 55.

11. United States, Department of the Interior, Bureau of Indian Affairs, "Report of the Commissioner of Indian Affairs," *Annual Reports of the Department of the Interior for the Fiscal Year Ended June 30, 1905. Indian Affairs. Part I* (Washington: Government Printing Office, 1906), 12.

12. Cary C. Collins, "Art Crafted in the Red Man's Image: Hazel Pete, the Indian New Deal, and the Indian Arts and Crafts Program at Santa Fe Indian School, 1932–1935," *New Mexico Historical Review*, Vol. 78, No. 4 (2003), 441-445.

13. "7 Stats About Working Women to Celebrate the Women's Bureau Centennial," *U.S. Department of Labor Blog*, https://blog.dol.gov/2020/06/05/7-stats-to-celebrate-the-womens-bureau-centennial (accessed Dec. 31, 2023).

14. Alice Kessler Harris, *Out to Work: A History of Wage-Earning Women in the United States*, 20th anniversary edition (Oxford; New York: Oxford University Press, 2003), 128.

15. This broad-brush account was distilled primarily from information from the following five sources: Tyrone D. Campbell, *Timeless Textiles:*

Traditional Pueblo Arts 1840–1940 (Santa Fe: Museum of Indian Arts and Culture, 2003); Nancy Fox, *Pueblo Weaving and Textile Arts* (Santa Fe: Museum of New Mexico Press, 1978); Kate Peck Kent, *Pueblo Indian Textiles: A Living Tradition* (Santa Fe: School of American Research Press, 1983); School for Advanced Research, *Pueblo Textiles and Embroidery* (video of public panel presentation at the New Mexico Museum of Art, Sept. 23, 2018), https://www.youtube.com/watch?v=kZ-3j31Jd2M (accessed June 30; July 1, 2, and 3, 2023); School for Advanced Research, *We Dance with Them: Pueblo Indian Embroidery*, https://www.sarweb.org/embroidery/default.htm (accessed Aug. 9, 2022); Kathleen Whitaker, *Southwest Textiles: Weavings of the Navajo and Pueblo* (Seattle: University of Washington Press, 2002).

16. The classic period was followed by the Anglo period (1880-1920) and, after that, the revival period.

17. Kent, *Pueblo Indian Textiles*, 12.

18. Thanks to Patrick Cruz of the Museum of Indian Arts and Culture in Santa Fe for vividly demonstrating this to me on a September morning in 2023 by pulling out drawer after drawer in the museum's textile storage area so that I could see classic-period Pueblo embroidery up close for myself.

19. As quoted in Sando, *Nee Hemish*, 190.

I
Beginnings

Mary Ellen Ross was born on June 26, 1871 in Ellis Prairie, Missouri, an unincorporated community in Texas County, in the Ozark Highlands, in the south-central part of the state. As a girl, she was known familiarly as "Mollie" (or "Molly"). After marriage, she dropped her first name and went by her middle name.

Mollie was the oldest of ten children of widower Samuel Lafayette Ross (1840–1910) and his second wife, Cassandra Kinkaid Slaughter Ross (1848-1949), who were married in Texas County on May 15, 1870. Samuel's first wife—Mahala Prigmore Ross (1845–1867)—and his second were both Missouri natives. Cassandra was born in Pineville in McDonald County in southwestern Missouri; in 1860, she lived with her family in Bonhomme in St. Louis County.

Samuel had come to Missouri as a boy. A son of farmer James Thomas Ross (1808–1892) and Sarah ("Sally") Cook Ross, he was born in Maryville, Blount County, Tennessee. James, Sally, and their children appear in Missouri in the federal census for 1850, indicating emigration from Tennessee sometime in the 1840s.

Ross is a Scottish surname common in Ulster Province in Ireland. Ellen Lawrence's Presbyterianism reflects the Scots-Irish origins of her father's family.

The area from which James Ross hailed lies in the foothills of the Smoky Mountains in the Appalachian Range of eastern Tennessee. Cherokee country prior to the influx of transatlantic immigrants in the eighteenth century, its population by the time James was born consisted heavily of descendants of Scots-Irish Presbyterians who came to North America seeking refuge. Their old-world ancestors left lowland Scotland for the north of Ireland through the eighteenth century and ultimately crossed the Atlantic to North America to escape economic hardship and religious oppression by the British. On the Tennessee frontier, they practiced their religion and sustained their families. Many became farmers. In the nineteenth century, in search of more and better land and a chance to elevate their prospects, their descendants chased the American frontier westward across the continent.[1]

Samuel Lafayette Ross was born in East Tennessee shortly after the 1838–1839 forcible removal of the Cherokee by the federal government from Tennessee to what is now Oklahoma over the infamous Trail of Tears. His father had lived in proximity with the Cherokee at a time of increasing federal determination to appropriate their land and to prevent retaliation for grievances. Did Ellen Lawrence's grandfather have complex feelings about the interaction of Indians and whites as a result of his situation? Did he share any thoughts he might have had on the subject with his granddaughter? In the absence of documentation, these questions remain unanswered—regrettably so, since answers to them might illuminate the degree to which Ellen's disposition toward Native Americans either echoed or diverged from inherited outlook.

Also undetermined is whether Samuel Lafayette Ross—Mollie's father—served in the Civil War, and if so, whether in the Union or Confederate Army. Soldiers from Missouri—a slave state and a border state—fought on both sides. Records of the two armies include soldiers with the not uncommon name Samuel Ross, but the detail they contain is insufficient to identify any of them with confidence as Ellen Lawrence's father. The subject is germane because Mollie eventually married a Georgia-born Confederate veteran. How steeped was she in southern attitudes about the capabilities and rights of non-whites?

When Samuel and Cassandra Ross began their married life in 1870, Sarah, James, and Thomas Ross—Samuel's three children by his first marriage, born in 1863, 1865, and 1867, respectively—were part of their household. Their family rapidly expanded to include Mollie and her younger siblings: Elizabeth (born 1873); Robert (niece Mildred's father; born 1875); Cyrus (1877); Porter (1879); Lena (1882); Edward (1884); Perry (1887); Estes (1891); and Annie (1894).

Like his father, Samuel Lafayette Ross was a farmer, first in Missouri, later in Texas. In 1870, the year he married Cassandra Slaughter, he, Cassandra, and his three children by Mahala lived in Township 55, Range 20, Chariton, Missouri—an unincorporated community in Putnam County, close to the Missouri-Iowa border. The Missouri state census places them in Township 31 in Texas County in 1876. By 1880, the growing family had moved to White Rock, a township in McDonald County, in the Ozark Plateau, close to Missouri's borders with Oklahoma and Arkansas and, coincidentally, also to the relocated Cherokee Nation. Two years later, in 1882, they left Missouri for Texas.

Eleven-year-old Mollie took with her an awareness of a Missouri weaving tradition that informed her later working life.

In a lengthy footnote to her history of the Albuquerque Indian School, where Ellen Lawrence taught in the 1930s, Lillie G. McKinney wrote, "Mrs. Ellen Lawrence learned colonial weaving in the Ozark mountains of Missouri when quite young."[2] The specificity and detail of that footnote in its entirety suggest that McKinney, whose history of the school was submitted in 1934 as a University of New Mexico master's thesis, obtained her information directly from Lawrence.

Decades after Ellen's death in 1965, artist Lucy Yepa Lowden—her student and protégée at the Albuquerque Indian School—also referred in interviews to her teacher's origins in the Ozarks in connection with her expertise in weaving.[3]

How and where young Mollie Ross became familiar with "colonial weaving" in Missouri are unknown. It is possible that Cassandra Ross was a weaver and that her oldest daughter observed her at the loom and learned by helping, or that some other relative practiced the craft. Regardless of how she became conscious of it, Appalachian/Ozark coverlet weaving was key to the blossoming not only of Mollie's interest in textile arts in general but also to her later appreciation of Pueblo textiles in particular. In its place in Appalachian and Ozark culture and the social circumstances surrounding its practice, it shared some fundamental similarities with traditional Pueblo weaving.

In the Appalachian region of the rural American south in the late eighteenth and early nineteenth centuries, professional weavers were primarily men, but women and girls turned out the fabric needed for household purposes.[4] A form of hand weaving combining a ground cloth and a pattern, overshot weaving was carried west as the frontier advanced, and thrived in the Ozarks as well as in the Appalachians. Incorporating hand-spun wool yarn colored with vegetable dyes, its distinctive products featured strong, repeating geometric designs.[5] Coverlets could be made by weaving strips of fabric on a four-harness loom and sewing them together. Designs were passed down within families and "shared within communities like a good recipe."[6]

The awareness of overshot coverlet weaving as rooted in history—a living inheritance from earlier generations—has been integral to its perpetuation. Coverlet collector Elene M. Combs commented in an interview with Kathleen Curtis Wilson, "We collect coverlets because it was instilled in me when I was young to appreciate the beauty and value of handmade things. The fact that my grandfather and mother were born into weaving families made this tenet all the more dear. Sharing keeps their work alive."[7] Modern-day weavers as well as collectors find a tangible link with the past in the handiwork of their predecessors. Part of their sense of mission arises from the near-loss of the craft, knowledge of which had declined by the turn of the twentieth century.[8]

Twenty-first century Pueblo weavers, too, are keenly conscious of their role in keeping the ancestral past alive in authentically-produced textiles. In a September 23, 2018 panel presentation offered by the School for Advanced Research in Santa Fe, Louie Garcia, Aric Chopito, and Isabel Gonzales discussed Pueblo weaving as an almost-lost art that modern practitioners have resuscitated through attention to oral tradition and the study of surviving specimens. Although concern over cultural appropriation may prevent modern Pueblo textile artists from sharing their knowledge of inherited design and technique beyond their communities, ensuring that knowledge of it does not die is nevertheless an overarching objective for them.[9]

Moreover, while the Appalachian women and girls who wove for their families did so for quotidian purposes, they nevertheless took pride in the artistry of their work, which was bold, vibrant, and varied, and they were moved by more than mere practicality in its creation. Kathleen Curtis Wilson has written, "Appalachian weavers did not put away their looms in the nineteenth century, but made a conscious decision to continue to weave beautiful objects for their own pleasure, as gifts for family members, or in celebration of important events."[10] After the rise of factory-made commercial cloth in the mid-nineteenth century, many women for whom overshot coverlet weaving was part of family heritage still practiced it even though there was no longer a necessity to do so—it satisfied an aesthetic hunger and a higher creative impulse.

In this, it resembled traditional Pueblo weaving, which was also produced primarily for internal use—for family and community ceremonies or for gift—rather than commercial, and in the making of which non-material considerations were as important as material. In writing about the Pueblo of Jemez, Joe Sando observed, "Religion continues to permeate all phases of community life" and contrasted the "essential spiritual outlook" of the Pueblos with the "materialistic standard of the dominant society."[11] This relates to Pueblo handicrafts as much as to any other aspect of Pueblo life. In the 2018 SAR panel discussion, Pueblo of Jemez textile artist Isabel Gonzales underscored the spiritual underpinning of Pueblo weaving by pointing out that the mere reproduction of ancient designs does not translate into the infusion of Pueblo prayers and hopes into woven products. The revival of endangered handicrafts is meaningless unless infused with spirit and reverence. Authenticity—adherence to traditional techniques and designs—solely to enhance salability degrades the woven product. A blanket is more than just a blanket.

Thus, when Ellen Lawrence first encountered Pueblo embroidery and the vestiges of Pueblo weaving at Jemez in 1919 and the 1920s, there was much about the way they embodied and reflected culture that would have resonated for her, despite differences in technique, equipment, material, and design between Native traditions and her own. Her early experience of handicraft in Missouri had nurtured sensitivity to subtle commonalities.

Samuel and Cassandra Ross's family increased in Texas. Their children Edward, Perry (who lived for just six days), Estes, and Annie were born there. Edward was born in San Saba County, in the center of the state, Estes and Annie in Hill County, northeast of San Saba. In 1900, Samuel and Cassandra lived in a rented home in Navarro County, which is east of Hill County. At the time of his death in January 1910, they lived farther north, in Wise County, near Decatur, the county seat, in a home that they owned without a mortgage, according to the widowed Cassandra's listing in the federal decennial census for that year.

As in Missouri, Mary Ellen Ross's father farmed to provide for his household. A brief notice in the *Wise County Messenger* for January 20, 1905 identifies cotton as among his crops: "S. L. Ross was in town Tuesday and stated that he and his neighbors would plant about half the amount of cotton they did last year. He very sensibly argues that it is better to raise five bales at 10 cents a pound than ten bales at 5 cents a pound, since the five bales do not cost near so much to produce as the ten bales and half the land required for the ten bales is saved to plant something else."[12] A practical man, evidently.

At his death in 1910, Samuel Ross was described as "an old-time citizen of this county...well and favorably known and...highly respected."[13] A

Freemason, he was buried with Masonic honors in the Jonestown Cemetery in Wise County. His widow remarried in 1916. Matthew Duke, Cassandra's second husband, died in 1922. She passed away in Willow, Oklahoma in 1949, at almost 101 years of age.

While her parents were growing and raising their family and putting food on the table in Texas, Mollie Ross was acquiring a basic education. She attended public elementary school as she had in Missouri and went on to high school in Hubbard, in Hill County, concluding her formal schooling there after three years—she did not earn a high school degree.[14] Concurrently, all on her own, she was learning a handicraft skill—the old-world folk art of lace making, which would, after marriage, provide her with an income stream, recognition for her proficiency, the opportunity to write a book, and her first job as a teacher of Native Americans.

Bobbin lace and needle lace comprise the two major categories of handmade lace, of which there are many varieties. Because lace enjoyed popularity as a component of fashion from the sixteenth into the early twentieth century, there was a market for it during this period. Bobbin lace is worked on a marked paper pattern attached to a special pillow. Bobbins (spools, typically made of wood, in earlier times of bone) hold twisted and braided lengths of thread for making lace. The thread is looped over pins at the top of the pattern, to which the finished portion of the lace-in-progress is pinned.

The history of this craft form was traced in the 1911 *Priscilla Bobbin Lace Book*, Ellen Lawrence's only published book: "The art of making lace with bobbins was invented about the middle of the sixteenth century. One hundred and fifty years later bobbin lace was made in practically all parts of Europe. The art was at its best from that time until about one hundred years ago. Machine-made lace almost ruined the sale of both needle and bobbin lace during the last century… During the last thirty years, the making of real lace has been revived in Europe, and now lace equal in every way to that made in the 'good old days' is being made and sold. Ladies all over the world are finding that machine…laces never equal, either in beauty or in durability, that made entirely by hand."[15] Bringing the waning handicraft of bobbin lace making back to life thus engaged Ellen Lawrence before she became involved in the revival of Pueblo weaving and embroidery.

The writer observed that "real lace" had never been made "to any extent" in America and lamented that "quantities of it are brought here from Europe. Much of this imported lace is of such poor quality that it could not find a purchaser in Europe."[16] Respect for both traditional methods of production and for quality went hand-in-hand for her well before she developed an interest in Pueblo textile crafts.

Self-teaching was presented as adequate to mastering bobbin lace making: "The fact that teachers of lace-making are seldom to be found in the United States has prevented many from learning the art. This book is written to fill the need for good instructions in making bobbin lace. It is much easier to learn to make bobbin lace than it is to learn to knit or to crochet. Personal lessons are not at all necessary."[17] In downplaying the importance of the mediator between handicraft and practitioner, Lawrence shared her knowledge without exaggerating her role.

At least two accounts affirm that Ellen, as a girl in Texas, taught herself lace making. Lillie McKinney wrote in her history of the Albuquerque Indian School, "She moved to Texas in 1882 and took up lace making by studying the designs and instruction in foreign books and magazines."[18] It can't have been easy for a girl of limited means to obtain such reading matter in rural Texas in the 1880s. Someone in her vicinity must have shared items from their personal bookshelves with the eager girl.

McKinney's measured academic account jibes with the chronology of Lawrence's life as presented in other documentation (in particular, with the timing of her move to Texas). Zahrah E. Preble had earlier painted a more journalistic picture in a biographical sketch of Ellen Lawrence as a lace teacher to Native Americans in California for *Sunset, the Pacific Monthly*, published a few months after Lawrence transferred to Jemez as a field matron. Preble possibly aimed to create an engaging narrative, with strict factuality a secondary consideration, or she was simply underinformed about the full details of Lawrence's life.

Like McKinney, Preble asserted that her subject taught herself lace making in Texas while young: "On a large, lonely ranch in Texas, a bright-eyed little girl of five watched her grandmother and aunt knitting, and begged to try it herself. They said she was too young to play with knitting needles, and besides, there was no extra money with which to buy them. But little Ellen had ideas that were different from other children. She had watched the hoar-frost on the window-panes, and the beautiful patterns penciled by Nature's fingers fascinated her. She wanted to capture those patterns. Her brother laughingly suggested that she use broom straws and she made serious selection of the firmest straws she could find…Because of her patient skill in working with broom straws, which bent and broke exasperatingly, she was rewarded with a pair of shining steel needles…When she was nine years old she watched a lady working on filet lace [a kind of needle lace] and later tried it out alone. When she was twelve she learned to do embroidery and eyelet work, but later came back to fine needle lace, drawing her own patterns when she couldn't buy or borrow lace to copy. When she was nineteen, a copy of a needle-work magazine fell into her hands, and she discovered that wonderful lace could be made with a pillow, plenty of pins, and little wooden bobbins wound with thread. She then whittled her own bobbins out of cedar wood."[19]

Except for chronology, McKinney's and Preble's accounts more or less agree. An Albuquerque newspaper article published just before Ellen Lawrence retired from the BIA in 1936 disorders the timeline to a somewhat greater degree in implying (though not overtly stating) that she learned lace making as well as weaving while very young in Missouri.[20]

The "needle-work magazine" Preble mentioned was in all likelihood *The Modern Priscilla*, a popular women's periodical that would later prove critical to the arc of Ellen Lawrence's career as a textile artisan and teacher. It began publication in 1887, three years before she turned nineteen.

1890 was a significant year for Mollie not only for her discovery of *The Modern Priscilla* but also for her entry into the work force as a country school teacher. BIA employees were periodically required (for performance evaluation, change of employment status, and other purposes) to fill out personal record blanks that included space for a summary of work history. BIA records filled out in Ellen Lawrence's tidy, legible manuscript hand show that she taught school in Texas between 1890 and her marriage in 1896 and again (after marriage and motherhood) from 1903 to 1904.[21] Moreover, a March 8, 1935 employment application related to a status change discloses that to qualify for teaching she had "more than twice 1890-1903" passed the Texas state teachers' examination.[22] She approached adulthood with both a practical means of earning a living and an established commitment to the craft occupations that would develop into her calling.

Somewhere along the way, Mollie Ross met Texas farmer Henry Harrison Lawrence, a man nearly thirty years her senior, born in Georgia on December 31, 1843. At a time when the life expectancy for an American man was shy of fifty years, the age difference between the two was noteworthy.[23] Nevertheless, they courted and, as announced in the column "Down Life Together" in the *Austin American-Statesman*, applied for a marriage permit in 1896.[24] Permit obtained, they married on September 10, 1896. Mollie Ross transformed into Ellen Lawrence, a farmer's wife in Oak Hill, Texas, an unincorporated community outside Austin, now within Austin city limits. As she assumed the responsibilities of her new role, she remained dedicated to textile handicrafts. By this point, she understood that the practice of handiwork was essential to her sense of satisfaction and purpose. More than that, it was embedded in her identity. Soon, it would become a means of making money.

NOTES

1. Inez E. Burns, *History of Blount County, Tennessee, from War Trail to Landing Strip, 1795-1955*, facsimile reprint of original 1957 edition, which

was sponsored by the Mary Blount Chapter, Daughters of the American Revolution, and the Tennessee Historical Commission (Westminster, Maryland: Heritage Books, 2011), Chapters I and II, 1-30; Billy Kennedy, *The Scots-Irish in the Hills of Tennessee* (Londonderry: Causeway Press, 1995), Chapter 2, 19-26.

2. Lillie G. McKinney, "History of the Albuquerque Indian School (Concluded) [Part 3]," *New Mexico Historical Review*, Vol. 20, No. 4 (Oct. 1945), footnote 58, 320.

3. Katherine Saltzstein, "Artist Helps Preserve Her Culture," *Albuquerque Journal*, Jan. 13, 1991, 26; Dean Balsamo, "Lucy Yepa Lowden gives insight into world of her 'little people'," *Santa Fe New Mexican*, June 12, 1992, 72.

4. Martha L. Benson and Laura Lyon Redford, *Ozark Coverlets: The Shiloh Museum of Ozark History Collection* (Springdale, Arkansas: Shiloh Museum of Ozark History, 2015), 8.

5. Missouri Historic Costume and Textile Collection, *Textiles in Time: The James Ray Coverlets*, edited by Laurel Wilson (Columbia: University of Missouri, 2009), 4.

6. "A Brief History of Overshot Weaving," article series "Overshot Weaving," *Comfortcloth*, https://comfortclothweaving.com/article/history-overshot-weaving (accessed Feb. 2, 2024).

7. Kathleen Curtis Wilson, *Textile Art from Southern Appalachia: The Quiet Work of Women* (Johnson City, Tennessee: Overmountain Press, 2001), 95.

8. Ibid., xi.

9. School for Advanced Research (Santa Fe), *Pueblo Textiles and Embroideries* (video of public panel presentation at the New Mexico Museum of Art, Sept. 23, 2018; moderator Brian Vallo, panelists Louie Garcia, Aric Chopito, and Isabel Gonzales), https://www.youtube.com/watch?v=kZ-3j31Jd2M (accessed June 30, July 1, 2, and 3, 2023).

10. Wilson, *Textile Art from Southern Appalachia*, x.

11. Sando, *Nee Hemish*, 205.

12. "S. L. Ross was in town…" [newspaper notice], *Wise County Messenger* (Decatur, Texas), Jan. 20, 1905, 5.

13. [S. L. Ross obituary], *Wise County Messenger*, Jan. 14, 1910, 5.

14. BIA personnel records, including (among other documents): Ellen Lawrence, completed personal record, June 7, 1915; completed personal information card, undated [July 1916]; Superintendent Reuben Perry, Albuquerque Indian School, efficiency record for EL, May 1, 1928. Although her federal census listing for 1940 suggests that EL completed four years of high school, multiple BIA records indicate otherwise.

15. Ellen Lawrence, *Bobbin Lace: Designs and Instruction*, 2nd edition (an "unabridged republication of the *Priscilla Bobbin Lace Book*...[of] 1911"), edited by Jules and Kaethe Kliot (Berkeley, California: Lacis Publications, 1989, copyright 1979), 3.

16. Ibid.

17. Ibid.

18. McKinney, "History of the Albuquerque Indian School (Concluded)," footnote 58, 320.

19. Zahrah Preble, [biographical sketch of Ellen Lawrence], "Interesting Westerners," *Sunset, the Pacific Monthly*, Vol. 42, No. 5 (May 1919), 46.

20. "Mrs. Lawrence was born in Missouri in the Ozarks and her earliest recollections are of weaving and lace making when she was barely old enough to hold a needle."—"She Taught Indians How to Weave, Revived Ancient Embroidery Designs," *Albuquerque Tribune*, May 30, 1936, 2.

21. BIA personnel records, Ellen Lawrence, completed, notarized personal statement of employee, Jan. 25, 1922; completed personal record blank, June 19, 1923.

22. Ibid., Ellen Lawrence, completed application for employment, Mar. 8, 1935.

23. "Life expectancy in the US, 1900-98," https://u.demog.berkeley.edu/~andrew/1918/figure2.html (accessed Nov. 7, 2023).

24. "Down Life Together" [listing of marriage permits issued during the week ending Sept. 12, 1896], *Austin American-Statesman*, Sept. 13, 1896, 3.

2
Farm Wife

The Lawrences began married life in 1896 under the cloud of nation-wide economic depression. Deflation, unemployment, and financial instability impacted the country. Often saddled with debt incurred through land purchase and borrowing to plant annual crops, farmers—particularly those in the south and west—keenly felt this crisis. Many favored the policy of unlimited coinage of silver—"free silver"—as the solution to their problems and advocated for it over the gold standard. Free silver would expand the money supply and raise inflation, they believed, making it easier to repay debts. This put them at odds with the financial "haves"—bankers, railroad magnates, landlords, factory and business owners—who upheld maintaining the more limited money supply that gold sustained. It also pitted the northeastern part of the country against the south and the west and urbanites against rural dwellers. Democrats and Populists embraced free silver, Republicans opposed it. Henry Harrison Lawrence—a Democrat and a farmer—supported free silver.[1]

On July 20, 1895 (a year before he married Mollie Ross), Henry Lawrence attended a free silver convention in Austin, Texas. As reported in the *Galveston Daily News*, the city was "political headquarters and…a number of the big chiefs of the free silver movement reside here."[2] The convention opened with "forty-eight men in the house beside reporters." At the peak of attendance during the day, there were approximately one hundred and fifty, of which "probably fifty were advocates of free silver, while the balance were republicans, both white and colored, populists and sound money men…But there was a good sprinkling of the free silver leaders present."

At noon, free silver advocates met to select delegates to the state convention in Fort Worth the following month. A committee of five was appointed "to select and submit to the convention a list of delegates to represent Travis county in the Fort Worth convention" on August 6. An amendment added three more members to the committee. J. S. Hogg (one of the three proposed) declined to serve, stating that "it would be better to place some country gentleman" in his stead. Albert S. Burleson suggested H. H. Lawrence, and the suggestion was adopted. Before the meeting was adjourned, the committee of eight recommended twenty-nine delegates. Among them were James Stephen ("Jim") Hogg, a Democratic former Texas attorney general and governor; Albert S. Burleson, a progressive Democrat who would later become a United States representative from Texas and United States postmaster general; and Henry Lawrence. Appreciation of Lawrence as a loyal and supportive Democrat is implicit in his placement on a committee that included some prominent Austin-area politicos.

His ties to the Confederacy may also have contributed to Lawrence's selection for the nominating committee and as a delegate to the 1895 free silver convention. Born in Forsyth County, Georgia to William Henry and Caroline Harrison Lawrence in 1843, Henry Harrison Lawrence fought for the Confederacy during the Civil War.[3] Like Georgia, Texas was a confederate state, and after the war it welcomed incomers from the south. Although he didn't leave much of a footprint to document his migration from Appalachian Georgia to Texas, in Texas he was part of a sizeable population of former southerners. Many arrived in Travis County in the 1870s, drawn by the availability of land and recent railroad construction. Those who had grown cotton back home found the climate and landscape around Austin suitable for the cultivation of this familiar crop.[4]

Party leaders like Hogg and Burleson, whose fathers had served as confederate officers, could feel confident in the allegiance of Travis County Democrats who had fought on behalf of the Confederacy. Such men rewarded shared ideology and political loyalty by advocating for local needs and through patronage. The Burleson connection later proved valuable to Henry Lawrence's wife. In March of 1915, preservationist Emma K. Burleson—Albert Burleson's sister—wrote a glowing letter of recommendation to

BIA Commissioner Cato Sells on behalf of Ellen Lawrence, who was then seeking a position with the BIA.[5]

In 1884, Oak Hill had seventy-five residents; by 1904, its population was two hundred. The community expanded during the 1880s with the construction in Austin of a new state capitol building, which utilized limestone quarried in the vicinity of Oak Hill and transported to the city via a railroad built for the purpose.[6] (An entry in the state capitol building payroll records for 1882-1888 lists an H. H. Lawrence as a laborer on the project in 1886—perhaps Henry Harrison Lawrence?[7]) Presumably attracted by the growth of this area in which pecans, cotton, wool, hides, and other agricultural commodities were produced, in late 1890 Henry Lawrence bought forty-three acres of land in Oak Hill of Joel Pearl for $215.[8] This was but one of the parcels he owned there.

Years later, the piece of property on which the farmhouse the Lawrences occupied stood was advertised for sale in the *Austin American*. The notice paints a picture of a place with good agricultural potential: "FOR SALE—27 acres of good level black land, one-half in cultivation, the other in wood and grass; good well of water and irrigated garden; 100 young fruit trees of different varieties; house on rural route 5; seven miles from Austin..."[9] His planting of fruit trees reflected Lawrence's optimism as he took up farm life on the outskirts of Austin. However, another, later advertisement listing the property for sale includes the cryptic comment "Not much house," hinting that his family may have lived austerely there.[10]

In the 1910 federal census, Lawrence's occupation was characterized as "General Farm," indicating that in addition to fruit he turned out other commonplace produce that ended up on kitchen and dining tables in Austin. His name was listed in a 1915 newspaper article about the response of thirty-eight Austin-area farmers to a proposal to experimentally employ the parcel post system "as a carrier of county produce to the homes of city consumers." This piece specifies a range of products offered by general farms in Travis County: "Nearly every one said that he could furnish butter and eggs and under the head of general produce is included pork, chickens, syrup, lard, turkeys, vegetables, sausage, home-made bread and fresh meats of different kinds."[11] The wives of the responding farmers were undoubtedly involved in the production of some of these farm commodities.

Ellen Lawrence likely maintained a henhouse for eggs and churned butter for market. Additionally, she supplemented the household income by selling goose feathers, as revealed in a 1912 advertisement in the *Austin American-Statesman*: "FOR SALE—Deodorized white goose feathers, 75c per pound. Call or address Mrs. H. H. Lawrence, Austin, R. F. D. No. 5."[12] Clean goose feathers would have been useful for making pillows and bedding.

Caring for her husband and child claimed much of Ellen Lawrence's time and attention while her family lived in Texas. The Lawrences' son was born in Oak Hill on August 27, 1899 and named after his father. In due course, he attended the Oak Hill School.[13] In June 1923, his mother summarized her life during her family's Texas years: "1896–1913, Housekeeper for my own family also dairymaid—laundress, seamstress etc. also practical nurse between other jobs."[14] The demands of her life required that she multitask.

In the first years of the twentieth century, the Lawrences attempted to offset money concerns by selling some of their land. In 1902, they sold the forty-three acres H. H. Lawrence had purchased of Joel Pearl in 1890 to Samuel Lafayette Ross, Ellen's father, for $800, nearly four times what Lawrence had paid for it.[15] They continued to reside at Oak Hill and to work this land after selling it. This was clearly a private arrangement that brought in cash while keeping the property within the family. They later came into possession of those forty-three acres again, likely at the death of Samuel Ross in 1910, and sold it in 1913, when they headed to California.[16]

Not long after the sale of property to her father, Ellen Lawrence took work outside her home to help make farm and household ends meet. Above the line in the June 19, 1923 personal information form in which she recorded working as a "country school teacher" from 1890 to her marriage, she inserted the addition "also in 1903–4."[17] Her son was still very young—four years old—at that point, which suggests that the Lawrences were strapped for cash.

While living in Oak Hill, Ellen Lawrence also relied upon her textile skills to generate income for household and farm. In addition to serving as helpmeet to her husband, raising her son, and teaching school, she maintained something of a cottage industry in lace and needlework, which she described tersely in her June 7, 1915 personal record form for the BIA: "1900–1913, made lace and embroidery for private customers."[18] Emma Burleson's March 1915 letter of recommendation for Lawrence confirmed the longevity of this enterprise: "For many years Mrs. Lawrence lived in Austin, Texas, earning her living by lace making."[19]

Beginning early in America's history, women had worked for hire in their own homes. From colonial times, textile products had been produced through the putting-out (or domestic) system, under which women were organized by a manufacturer or agent to fulfill work orders at home.[20] From the mid-nineteenth century on, as factory production and efficiency burgeoned, the putting-out system grew increasingly exploitative and brought diminishing returns to contracted workers.[21]

In Texas, Ellen Lawrence followed in the tradition of women remotely producing textile products intended for sale, but her wording on her 1915 BIA form seems to indicate that she was her own agent—that she worked on direct order for the customers who wanted to purchase her handiwork. Although there is no way of knowing whether she was paid fairly for her time and skill, as an independent agent she would have had more control over compensation and other particulars than did women hired by an intermediary between customer and producer. That it was worthwhile for her to keep this venture going for more than a decade implies that she managed it successfully. Her familiarity with *The Modern Priscilla*—the women's needlework publication that she had discovered as a teenager and that multiple BIA documents reveal she read faithfully during her career in the Indian Service—probably raised her awareness of how to market her work.

Established in 1887 in Lynn, Massachusetts and published in Boston from 1894, *The Modern Priscilla* was a popular magazine issued by the Priscilla Publishing Company. It focused on sewing, fancy work, china painting, cookery, and other topics relating to homemaking and women's lives. The periodical featured patterns and instructions for making a range of items and sponsored contests for best of kind in different categories. The Priscilla Publishing Company also issued a series of topical how-to books on specific handicrafts represented in its magazine.

Early twentieth-century issues of *The Modern Priscilla* include advertisements for schemes by which women might work from home on something resembling a putting-out basis, allowing them to earn money without stepping beyond the traditional boundaries of their sphere.[22] They include, too, articles about other means by which craftswomen could market handmade articles—women's exchanges or salesrooms in urban centers, for instance, to which completed work could be sent. The author of one article observed, "It means much to a woman in a country village, where there are long hours to be passed alone without sufficient to occupy her hands, to know that these hours may be profitably employed in the making of some article which can be sent hundreds of miles away, there to find a purchaser; for while in their home town there is no demand for the fine needlework, the dainty articles of wear, either sewed, knitted, or crocheted, in the larger cities the demand exceeds the local supply."[23]

Living on the edge of a population center (Austin's population was close to 29,900 in 1910), Ellen Lawrence appears to have found customers for her lace and embroidery without relying on an external apparatus. Still, she must have known from reading *The Modern Priscilla* of the challenges faced by other women hoping for compensation for the time, effort, and materials invested in their handiwork.

The California Indian women whom Lawrence later taught to make bobbin lace as a means of earning income were, unlike their teacher, obliged to market their products through outside mechanisms. Nevertheless, they shared with her the fundamental similarity of harnessing craft skills to meet financial need. Lawrence had more in common with them than did many of the more affluent philanthropic women involved in elevating Native lives through arts and crafts initiatives in the early twentieth century. Having had to cope with some level of financial insecurity herself, she could approach the teaching of income-generating skills empathetically and practically. She was not driven by the sense of cultural and social superiority and prerogative that underlay the efforts of some of the other Anglo women she encountered along the way, among them Cordelia Sterling, who was central to Lawrence's early work in California as a lace teacher.

Between her marriage and her family's departure from Texas, Ellen Lawrence further developed and refined her lace and needlework skills. In addition, she capitalized on channels for communicating with others who shared her craft interests. The Priscilla Publishing Company was a particularly useful connection in this.

Zahrah Preble wrote of Lawrence's original pattern-making for lace during the time she lived in Oak Hill, "After marrying H. H. Lawrence, she continued working out original patterns in her Texas ranch home and disposing of them to a publisher."[24] By 1910, Lawrence's appearance as an author on the pages of *The Modern Priscilla* had created some name recognition for her beyond the Austin area as an expert in textile handicrafts. Her piece "Bow in Irish Crochet," for instance, appeared in the issue for April 1910, under the byline "By Ellen Lawrence."[25] The byline is significant—not all pieces in *The Modern Priscilla* were attributed. Its inclusion permitted the writer to cultivate a reputation.

There is some irony in the importance of *The Modern Priscilla* to Ellen Lawrence. The magazine played a prominent role in situating needlework within the colonial revival movement of the late nineteenth and early twentieth centuries. Colonial revivalists looked to an idealized past—a simpler, nobler time—in response to the problems and dissatisfactions of the present. They saw colonial artifacts and motifs as reflective of the qualities they attached to the period. They aimed at the preservation and interpretive reproduction of colonial architecture, home furnishings, housewares, clothing and more, and engaged in reenactments of various kinds.[26]

The movement was expressed at its outset in heightened awareness of their heritage on the part of those with colonial ancestry and in their demonstration of pride in colonial family artifacts, needlework and textiles included. In regards to textiles specifically, the revival developed into an organized Progressive effort by relatively advantaged social reformers who found virtue in America's early history to provide training and employment for disadvantaged and immigrant women in producing colonial-inspired handiwork, thereby imparting national values and bettering their financial situations. Ultimately, it led to a popularization among middle class women of prepackaged, mass-produced textile projects incorporating colonial motifs—a democratization of sorts. Over this trajectory, the crafter was deskilled and the product devalued. *The Modern Priscilla* was not the only women's needlework publication that promoted colonial revivalism, but it was a well-known and widely disseminated one.[27]

The irony in Ellen Lawrence's embrace of this publication arises from the reverence it encouraged for an elite, largely northeastern pedigree she herself did not possess and from its ultimate undercutting of high proficiency in skills by which she defined herself. And yet, in its revivalism, it reinforced her existing inclination to appreciate handiwork techniques and materials of the past. As it turned out, the textile revival in which she later participated in New Mexico was based on traditions centuries older than those celebrated by American coverlet weavers, colonial revivalists, and lace makers.

1911 was an important year in Ellen Lawrence's life as a craftswoman. An advertisement for her forthcoming book appeared on the inside of the front cover of the November issue of *The Modern Priscilla*:

> **NEW** Priscilla Bobbin Lace Book—**Out Dec. 1st** The growing interest in Bobbin Lace has induced us to issue this new volume in the series of Priscilla Needlework Books. It is edited by Ellen Lawrence, an expert in bobbin lace, whose lessons in this fascinating work, published in The Modern Priscilla, have aroused so much interest.

The lessons in the book take up the work from the beginning, all the tools and materials being fully described. Beautiful designs are given for Torchon, Cluny, Russian and Bruges laces, and include edges and insertions, doilies, medallions, handkerchiefs, etc., all illustrated from real work. The lessons are thoroughly practical, and have been arranged with especial reference to the beginner, although advanced lace-makers will find the designs attractive and useful.

Send your order at once and make sure of one of these exceptional books.[28]

The price for this thirty-six page title was twenty-five cents, postpaid.

The publication of her book opened up possibilities in Ellen Lawrence's later working life, bringing competitively awarded opportunities within her reach. A late 1914 memorandum regarding her desire to take a Civil Service examination to qualify for BIA employment after working on a temporary basis in California quotes from a letter written by Cordelia Sterling on June 23, 1913: "She...is the most expert lace-maker in America, and knows of every variety of lace and has written the books on lace-making for the Prisella [sic] Company of Boston."[29] The Priscilla connection conferred on Lawrence an advantage as a candidate.

Even before the *Priscilla Bobbin Lace Book* appeared, the Lawrences were looking to leave their Texas farm behind and make a fresh start elsewhere. At the age of seventy, Henry Lawrence must have lacked the physical vigor to keep the operation running. Moreover, the couple had had a hard time making a go of it, with little to show for their exertions.

As early as 1909, Ellen Lawrence hoped to procure employment in the BIA. Her BIA personnel files include a copy of an intriguing August 10, 1909 letter from Commissioner of Indian Affairs Robert Grosvenor Valentine to United States Senator from Kansas Charles Curtis, who was involved in Indian matters in several capacities and was himself a member of the Kaw Nation. Valentine wrote, "I have taken up the case of Mrs. Lawrence as I told you I would...and find no way of making any change at the present. The plan I had in mind...proved to be impossible...I shall keep the matter and your interest in it and mine before me and do the best I can."[30] Whatever behind-the scenes political maneuvering was responsible for bringing Ellen Lawrence to the attention of these two powerful men, she did not obtain the desired position for several more years.

In 1912, Ellen Lawrence applied unsuccessfully for the BIA position of lace teacher to Indian women in Pala, California.[31] In 1913, on behalf of the Redlands Indian Association, Cordelia Sterling arranged for her employment in California to teach lace making, her salary to be paid and the distribution and sale of her students' work to be managed through a public/private partnership between the BIA and private philanthropies.[32] This strategy relieved the federal government of the responsibility of fully supporting projects to improve the lives of Native people.

Henry and Ellen Lawrence pulled up stakes, selling three tracts of their farm property in Oak Hill in September 1913.[33] The relocation of their family to California and Ellen's assumption of work duties outside her home profoundly altered the dynamics of their marriage. From their departure from Texas until Henry Harrison Lawrence's death—a period of some thirteen years—his wife was the breadwinner. Although her work encompassed activities that were accepted in Anglo culture as woman's work, their relationship no longer reflected traditional gender roles. She was, essentially, the head of their household in all but name.

NOTES

1. California voter registrations for 1900-1968 on *Ancestry* confirm his party affiliation; he and Ellen lived in Riverside County, California, during the second half of the 1910s.

2. "Silver Convention. Ex-Governor Hogg Makes a Characteristic Speech and Declares for Free Silver. Lubbock and Col. Mills. Free Silver Convention in Austin to Select Delegates to the State Convention in Fort Worth Next Month," *Galveston Daily News*, July 20, 1895, 4.

3. The 1910 federal census identifies him as a veteran of the Confederate Army.

4. Austin, Texas, Historic Preservation Office, "A Short History of the Cotton Industry in Travis County," typescript, prepared by Steve Sadowski, Oct. 2018, [1] (accessible via Internet search as a PDF; accessed Feb. 25, 2024).

5. BIA personnel records, Emma K. Burleson, autograph letter, signed, Austin, Texas, Mar. 12, 1915, to Cato Sells (Washington, DC).

6. Vivian Elizabeth Smyrl, "Oak Hill TX (Travis County), *Handbook of Texas Online* (published by the Texas State Historical Association), https://www.tshaonline.org/handbook/entries/oak-hill-tx-travis-county (accessed Sept. 27, 2023); Mary Starr Barkley, *History of Travis County and Austin, 1839-1899*, second edition (Austin: Steck Company, 1967, copyright 1963), 203.

7. "H H Lawrence," Texas, U.S., Capitol Building Payroll, 1882-1888, *Ancestry*, https://www.ancestry.com/search/collections/2176/?name=H+H_Lawrence&event=1886 (accessed Feb. 26, 2024).

8. Notice of sale of land by Joel Pearl to H. H. Lawrence, "Real Estate Transfers," *Austin American-Statesman*, Dec. 14, 1890, 13.

9. "Real Estate for Sale," *Austin American*, Sept. 19, 1915, 10.

10. "Real Estate—," *Austin American-Statesman*, Aug. 15, 1923, 9.

11. "Farmers Respond to Postmaster; Offer Produce. Lists of Those Who Have Stuff to Sell," *Austin American-Statesman*, Mar. 7, 1915, 19.

12. "For Sale," *Austin American-Statesman*, May 28, 1912, 6; May 30, 1912, 7.

13. "Oak Hill School," *Austin American-Statesman*, Dec. 14, 1914, 6. Henry Lawrence was one of two student reporters for this piece, in which he is noted as having delivered a "splendid declamation" at the Dec. 4,

1914 meeting of the Oak Hill Educational League before a house "filled to its fullest capacity with the parents and others interested in the school."

14. BIA personnel records, Ellen Lawrence, completed personal record blank, June 19, 1923.

15. Notice of sale of land by "H. H. Lawrence and wife to S. L. Ross," "Real Estate Transfers," *Austin American-Statesman*, Oct. 13, 1902, 3.

16. Notice of sale of land by "H. H. Lawrence and wife to J. H. Langsford and wife," "Real Estate," *Austin American-Statesman*, Sept. 30, 1913, 6.

17. BIA personnel records, Ellen Lawrence, completed personal record blank, June 19, 1923.

18. BIA personnel records, Ellen Lawrence, completed personal record, June 7, 1915.

19. BIA personnel records, Emma K. Burleson, autograph letter, signed, Austin, Texas, Mar. 12, 1915, to Cato Sells (Washington, DC).

20. Kessler-Harris, *Out to Work*, 17-19.

21. Ibid., 149-150.

22. See, for example, an ad in the Nov. 1911 issue (page 50): "Work at Home Weaving Rugs and Carpet. No Experience Needed. $4 a Day Easily Made. We start men and women in a profitable business on a small investment. Write quick for prices and Loom Book. Reed Mfg. Co. Box W. Springfield, Ohio."

23. Mary Madeline Wood, "Marketing the Home Woman's Product," *The Modern Priscilla*, Vol. XXV, No. 7 (Sept. 1911), 48.

24. Preble, [biographical sketch of Ellen Lawrence].

25. Ellen Lawrence, "Bow in Irish Crochet," *The Modern Priscilla*, Vol. XXIV, No. 2 (Apr. 1910), 53, 59.

26. Mary Miley Theobald, "The Colonial Revival: The Past That Never Dies," *Colonial Williamsburg Journal*, Vol. 24, No. 2 (Summer 2002), 81-84.

27. Beverly Gordon, "Spinning Wheels, Samplers, and the *Modern Priscilla*:

The Images and Paradoxes of Colonial Revival Needlework," *Winterthur Portfolio*, Vol. 33, No. 2/3 (Summer-Autumn 1998), 163-194.

28. [Advertisement for *The Priscilla Bobbin Lace Book*], *The Modern Priscilla*, Vol. XXV, No. 9 (Nov. 1911), [2].

29. BIA personnel records, as quoted in typed memorandum to "Education Employees," Nov. 25, 1914.

30. BIA personnel records, Commissioner of Indian Affairs [Robert Grosvenor Valentine], typed letter, carbon copy, Washington, DC, Aug. 10, 1909, to Senator Charles Curtis (Washington, DC).

31. BIA personnel records, Acting Commissioner of Indian Affairs C. F. Hauke, typed letter, signature stamped, [Washington, DC], Sept. 26, 1912, to Ellen Lawrence (R.F.D. 5, Austin, Texas).

32. Redlands Indian Association, manuscript minute book, 1904-1928, Albert K. Smiley Public Library, Redlands, California, minutes from Nov. 26, 1912-Dec. 10, 1913. Regarding government collaboration with the Sybil Carter Indian Lace Association: Ellen Lawrence, autograph letter, signed, San Jacinto, California, Apr. 30, 1918, to Superintendent H. E. Wadsworth, Soboba Agency (San Jacinto), United States, Department of the Interior, Bureau of Indian Affairs, Record Group 75, Soboba Superintendency, Correspondence, 1907-1920, Lace Making Class, 1916-1918, Box 8, Folder 8, National Archives, Riverside; Preble, [biographical sketch of Ellen Lawrence].

33. Notice of sale of land by "H. H. Lawrence and wife to J. H. Langsford and wife."

3
Lace Teacher

Late nineteenth-century Christian missionary groups took on the creation of work opportunities for Native Americans to promote economic self-reliance and rapid assimilation into the white world, their efforts dovetailing with BIA objectives. At that time, the BIA approached Native handicrafts largely through a market-oriented lens, and charitable organizations followed suit. Superintendent of Indian Schools Estelle Reel wrote of basket making in her 1901 *Course of Study for the Indian Schools of the United States*: "The basketry woven by Indians for generations past is fast becoming a lost art and must be revived by the children of the present generation, that they may take their rightful place among the leading basket makers of the world and supply the demands of the markets for such baskets."[1]

In reporting specifically on lace making more than a decade later, BIA Commissioner Cato Sells maintained this earlier emphasis on earning income as a major purpose of handicraft activity: "Lace making is becoming a very important industry in some localities, especially among the Mission Indians in Southern California. This industry...enables women and children to utilize their spare time in the home and derive from their labors an income to aid in their support."[2] He underscored the substantial amount of money generated by blanket weaving, basket making, pottery, lace making, and beadwork and highlighted the priority of doing "everything possible to encourage the Indians to improve the products of native industries, so as to make the articles produced very largely of a useful and practical sort, and then to find the best market for disposing of the products to the best advantage for the Indians."

Philanthropic industrial and handicraft initiatives did not necessarily take into account the traditions of the Natives they aimed to elevate. In the words of Robert Fay Schrader, "Although basically humanitarian in concept, these efforts were designed to help the Indians become white people, and exhibited no concern for the preservation of the crafts or the culture that produced them."[3] Teaching Native Americans to make lace—an eminently European handicraft—was among such well-intended and remunerative but culturally dubious undertakings.

The profitability of Native American lace making declined as the product fell out of vogue.[4] It was impacted, too, by the First World War, which put an end to importation of European linen thread and the steel pins needed for making bobbin lace.[5]

Native women learned lace making through a combination of BIA and private efforts. The work of the Women's National Indian Association played a significant role in promoting this handicraft. Established in 1879 to support the Christianization and assimilation of Native American people, the WNIA advocated on behalf of a variety of measures intended to advance Native rights and protection. Headquartered in Philadelphia, the national organization encouraged the formation of state and branch associations and more informal local Indian committees to implement its goals.

In 1891, Amelia Stone Quinton—president of the WNIA—founded an Indian committee in Redlands, California, which in 1894 organized as the Redlands Indian Association. The RIA directed efforts to aiding the Mission Indians in its vicinity, "touring their villages, sending Christmas boxes, educating the public on Indian issues, and supporting missionaries, government field matrons, and schoolteachers."[6] The association also backed the production and marketing of handicraft items made by Indians, lace among them. The RIA separated from the WNIA in 1910 and subsequently put energy and funding into lace making at the Pala

Indian Reservation in northern San Diego County. It was responsible for bringing Ellen Lawrence to California in 1913 to teach lace making to the Mission Indians.

The Sybil Carter Indian Lace Association partnered with the federal government and with private organizations in the production and distribution of lace made by Native American women across the country—southern California included—in the early twentieth century. Carter was a special agent for the Episcopal Board of Missions. In the course of her work, she learned to make lace from an English woman who had been abandoned by her husband. She later observed students at a lace school in Japan. Carter was moved by the poverty of Native American women. It dawned on her that they also could earn money through lace making. Convinced that the handicraft would "solve many questions which have been problems to us heretofore," she reported at the 1890 Lake Mohonk Conference of Friends of the Indian on her own experience of teaching lace making to Indian women.[7] In 1904, her friends formed the Sybil Carter Indian Mission and Lace Industry Association to purchase materials, arrange and pay for teachers, and transport and market the lace made on reservations to East Coast consumers.

The RIA and the Sybil Carter Lace Association worked collaboratively. Both were involved in the disposition of lace produced by Ellen Lawrence's Native students in California in the second decade of the twentieth century.[8]

Cordelia Sterling (wife of wealthy pressed brick inventor and manufacturer Edward Canfield Sterling) was president of the RIA on November 26, 1912, when the association met at her Redlands mansion, "La Casada," an elegant and manicured showplace in the San Bernardino Valley.[9] That meeting encompassed a discussion of creating work for the Pala Indians and a report by the president—who had interest and background in hand-produced lace—on "what might be done for them along the lines of lace making." The BIA had secured a lace teacher at Pala, a position for which Ellen Lawrence had applied but which was awarded to another applicant (Mrs. Edla C. Osterberg).[10] The RIA voted to "use the money in

Much to Learn, Much to Give

the treasury to aid in this work." Under this arrangement, the teacher was paid by the government but supervised by the RIA, while the furnishing of equipment and thread, the provision of funding to pay the Indians for their piecework, and the distribution and marketing of the product were privately managed.[11] (In some other places, the cost of the teacher was also privately funded, as BIA Commissioner Cato Sells indicated in his 1915 annual report.[12])

Cordelia Sterling had been inspired as a traveler in Italy by schools where women learned to make lace, to weave, or to embroider, and subsequently practiced their particular craft at home. The requisite supplies were provided to them and their handiwork was priced by committee, with the cost of materials subtracted, and finished items were sold in established shops or centers.[13] While abroad, Sterling made lace hands-on.

Like Sybil Carter, she was troubled by "the problem of the Indian woman left bewildered and helpless in the modern conditions surrounding her in the land of her fathers." She set about introducing a system similar to the Italian on reservations in southern California.[14] She communicated with the BIA about providing a lace teacher at Pala and saw to the establishment of association committees to facilitate and manage Indian lace making.

In the months following its November 1912 meeting, the RIA worked to implement and refine the mechanisms through which its commitment to Indian lace making might be fulfilled. At a meeting of its executive board on December 18, 1912, President Sterling "described at length the advantages to the Indians at the 18 reservations in this part of the state which would result from the introduction of lace making," after which the board discussed two important practical matters—"How to obtain the best material for this industry and how to dispose of the lace when made."[15] It was voted that the president appoint a committee to address supplies and sales.

The minutes of full member and executive board meetings for late 1912 and 1913 document the range of the RIA's involvement with Indian lace making. They cover progress made at Pala, where the president traveled with some frequency; growing interest in the craft and its possible extension to other reservations; the financial challenge of paying Indian women up front for the lace they made as it was completed without knowing whether it would sell quickly (the incurrence of debt was a concern); a visit by the Pala lace teacher and two of her students, who provided a demonstration; talks on and exhibits of Indian-made lace; considerations of pricing; committee work to investigate the sale of lace; donations to the RIA toward funding lace making; a trip to Los Angeles by Cordelia Sterling and Mrs. Jennie Davis to explore the potential sale of Indian lace through the stores there; and more.

The minutes for the April 26, 1913 meeting reveal some concern about the profitability of lace making: "The report was very discouraging as to the sale of torchon lace at this time, the fashion having gone out. We cannot compete with European prices, where there laces can now be bought very low. Filet and Cluny laces and doilies will now be introduced rapidly for making."[16] On November 3 of that year, Cordelia Sterling "presented a plan by which it was proposed to segregate the lace work from the other work of the Association."[17] At the December 10, 1913 annual meeting, a motion was made to do so: "[A]s Mrs. Sterling had given a great deal of time to the lace work, and had made herself responsible for its success, the work should be separated from the other activities of the Asso. and left entirely in the hands of Mrs. Sterling."[18] The motion was seconded and carried unanimously, and satisfaction in the progress of lace work at Pala to that point expressed.

The separation of this work from the RIA's other activities apparently developed out of anxiety over the amount of money and time necessary to advance lace making and the uncertainty of its ultimately proving gainful. It probably also reflected awareness that the forward momentum of RIA objectives overall could easily be derailed by the determination of a particularly strong and assertive individual member with her own special interests and agenda. In any case, Indian lace making at Pala became fully Cordelia Sterling's to manage.

Against the background of this mosaic of agencies, forces, and personalities, Ellen Lawrence went to California at the age of forty-two to teach Mission Indians to make lace. Between November 1913 and December 1914, she worked at the Soboba Reservation in San Jacinto (Riverside County) under the direction of Cordelia Sterling and Mrs. J. E. Davis of the RIA.[19]

During Lawrence's first months as a teacher of Native Americans, the lace-making women at Soboba agitated for a wage increase. A short article about their protest appeared in the *Los Angeles Times* and was reprinted in the *Indian School Journal* for April 1914. The first paragraph, in which the strike is reported, opens, "Redlands society women have been having a strike on their hands." The emphasis is front and center on the managers of the lace making operation. The last sentence of the paragraph draws attention to one of these society women in particular: "Mrs. E. C. Sterling, who is in charge of the lace making department of the Redlands Indian Society, returned from an emergency call to the reservation, where she succeeded in patching up the difficulty."[20]

The second and final paragraph includes an incidental reference to their teacher, who is not a particular focus of the piece:

> The Redlands Indian Society has just spent $1000 teaching the Soboba Indian women how to make lace. Most of the money was furnished by Mrs. Willis James of New York, said to be one of the wealthiest women in the United States. A teacher was employed to instruct the women. The society has furnished all the equipment necessary for lace making and contracted to take all the lace from the Indian women as soon as it is finished at prices ranging from 35 cents a yard upward.

Lawrence is not even named here.

The class consciousness implicit in this account is conspicuous. It bespeaks an underlying sense that the relatively affluent philanthropists in the story were more noteworthy than the teacher they supervised. In this, it foreshadows the development of friction and resentment between the subordinate Lawrence and the more privileged Sterling. This tension would bubble over in time.

Ellen Lawrence's working arrangement with the RIA expired in November 1914. She was allowed to continue working on a temporary basis until a permanent BIA position might open up. Before making application, she had to take the Civil Service examination to qualify for permanent federal employment.

Whatever sense of social superiority Sterling and her RIA colleagues possessed, Harwood Hall—a key BIA official with whom Ellen Lawrence came into contact during this period—championed the lace teacher as a valuable asset. Even before the RIA's initial involvement in overseeing Lawrence's work concluded, BIA Commissioner Cato Sells was considering the extension of lace teaching from Pala and Soboba to various other reservations under the Soboba and Malki jurisdictions. He solicited the opinion of Hall, who was Superintendent of the Soboba Agency, which included the Soboba, Cahuilla, Santa Ynez, Mesa Grande, Santa Rosa, and Santa Ysabel reservations. Hall pronounced the proposal "a good idea" and offered his assessment of Lawrence as a candidate for the potential job:

> Mrs. Lawrence, present teacher, is willing to compete in a regular examination, altho', naturally, she is not impressed with the idea of a reduction from $75. to $50. per month, for she is recognized as one of the leading experts in lace making in America, beside she is admirably adapted to work in the Indian service on account of her splendid disposition and influence for upbuilding the Indians in a better home and moral life.[21]

Ellen Lawrence subsequently took the Civil Service examination (she scored a 98), Emma Burleson sent her glowing letter of recommendation for the candidate to Cato Sells, and the hoped-for permanent position was awarded.[22] Lawrence assumed it in June 1915.

Harwood Hall again waxed eloquent on Lawrence's virtues later that year, when Edla Osterberg resigned as lace teacher at Pala and Commissioner Sells wanted to know from his California superintendents whether they thought Lawrence capable of taking on lace teaching at Pala and other reservations. Hall wrote Thomas F. McCormick, his colleague in the Pala superintendency, on October 14, 1915:

> I believe Mrs. Lawrence can do the work to the satisfaction of all concerned at all of the points mentioned...She is a hard worker, loyal and cooperates with everybody, and you would like her, for she attends to her own business strictly and supports the superintendent and the Indian work generally. Indeed, I feel that for the good of the lace making activity Mrs. Lawrence is the right person to take up the instruction as suggested by Mr. Sells. She is a woman of fine qualities, good common sense, with no frills, but just "saws wood," and is a positive help in keeping down any friction, instead of creating it.[23]

Hall's enthusiasm had its desired effect in the appointment of Ellen Lawrence as lace teacher to the Malki, Pala, and Campo superintendencies as well as at Soboba by mid-November 1915, with her headquarters remaining at Soboba.[24] She was required to report monthly to the office of the BIA commissioner through Hall at Soboba. She was also expected to continue cooperating with Cordelia Sterling. Even though she was no longer under Sterling's direction, Commissioner Sells advised, "She should consult with Mrs. Sterling frequently whenever it is convenient for Mrs. Sterling to visit her classes, or by correspondence, so that she may receive the valuable suggestions which Mrs. Sterling may be able to give from time to time."[25] In December, Lawrence's salary was increased from $600 to $720 yearly.[26]

Ellen Lawrence with California lace-making Indians. *Sunset, the Pacific Monthly* (May 1919).

Although difficulties in the relationship between Lawrence and Cordelia Sterling would arise soon enough, Sterling initially expressed support for Lawrence's assumption of expanded responsibilities. In a December 1915 letter to Thomas McCormick, she wrote comparing the new teacher at Pala to the former: "I do not feel able to keep up in the way Mrs. Osterberg carried on the work—Her books & accounts amounted to no account at all—I think Mrs. Lawrence will do differently, as she understands the business side of the question."[27] She went on in the same letter to note Ellen Lawrence's ability to make wooden bobbins—a useful and teachable skill, from Sterling's perspective—and to recommend that each student make her own bobbins as an alternative to their purchase, which she did not want to fund.

The logistics of teaching at geographically scattered reservations were arduous. Transportation took significant time and energy. The Pala superintendent detailed its complexities in a letter to Cato Sells on October 18, 1915:

> The outline for my jurisdiction would be to have Mrs. Lawrence make her first stop in Pechanga. She could be brought there by government conveyance from San Jacinto [where the Soboba Agency was headquartered] or come on the train to Temecula and then by government conveyance to Pechanga a distance of six miles. From Pechanga to San Jacinto is about forty miles. From Pechanga she would come to Pala by government conveyance a distance of eight miles.
>
> From Pala to Rincon a distance of twelve miles. From Rincon she would have to return to Pala and take the auto stage to Oceanside a distance of twenty-five miles. From Oceanside by rail to San Diego a distance of forty-five miles and from San Diego either by rail or auto stage to Lakeside a distance of about twenty miles. From Lakeside to Capitain Grande by government conveyance a distance of twelve miles. From Capitain Grande she would have to return to [L]akeside and thence by auto stage to Campo a distance of about sixty miles. From Campo on return trip to San Jacinto she would go by auto stage to San Diego a distance of sixty miles and from San Diego to [S]an Jacinto by rail a distance of one hundred and seventy-five miles.
>
> Regarding the trip from Pala to Capitain Grande I am sure that I can so arrange my work so as to be able to take Mrs. Lawrence to Capitain Grande most of the time and probably all the time. I believe if each superintendent interested will do his share a considerable amount of the expense can be avoided. The trip to Campo I believe can be made cheaper by auto stage than by government conveyance.[28]

This taxing itinerary likely caused Ellen Lawrence discomfort and inconvenience. It also regularly left Henry Lawrence on his own for periods of time, raising the question of how he managed his life while his wife was away from San Jacinto. The couple's teenage son presumably provided his father—who turned seventy-two in December 1915—with companionship and assistance.[29]

Beyond her regular lace teaching duties, the BIA called on Ellen Lawrence to demonstrate her craft at continuing education sessions for agency employees. She and Edla Osterberg (then still teaching at Pala) both presented at the two-week Sherman Institute in Riverside, California, in July 1914. Their program attracted so many registrants that the class had to be divided, "Mrs. Osterberg taking the class in bobbin lace and Mrs. Lawrence the class in filet work."[30] In the summer of 1916, Lawrence presented at Sherman again and also at the Salem School in Chemawa, Oregon.[31] Lawrence's instruction in lace making proved popular at Sherman that year, too. It was reported in the *Riverside Daily Press*, "A large number of the ladies became interested in the art of lace making as taught by Mrs. Ellen Lawrence, of Soboba, Cal."[32]

Lawrence's more extensive scope of action enhanced the visibility of her work and its public relations value to the BIA. In October 1916, Mrs. Salvadora Valenzuela—one of Ellen Lawrence's bobbin lace students at Pala—demonstrated her craft at the Riverside County Fair on October 12, 1916. She was described in a local newspaper article as "the center of an admiring crowd" and her dexterity was noted.[33] Valenzuela's teacher was explicitly mentioned and some details were given about the classes at Pala:

> This lace maker is a pupil of Mrs. Ellen Lawrence, who teaches the art at the Pala and Soboba reservations. School girls from the ages of eight years are being taught the fascinating art with the hope that it may be a means of income to them. There are between 20 and 30 girls and women in the Pala class, and the pupils do their work in spare moments after school or in their homes when their housework is finished.

The BIA Commissioner could not have asked for better press.

There are signs in Cordelia Sterling's late 1915 and early 1916 correspondence with Superintendent McCormick at Pala of a problematic hauteur that colored her dealings with the Native people for whom she professed concern, a sense of self-importance and knowing best that undermined her best intentions. In mid-December, 1915, she wrote McCormick about the character-building value to the California Indians of making their own bobbins for lace making:

> The best & I think the way I shall pursue, is to have them make their own. The men have plenty of time to do it for the women & children—I know of no community where there is so large an idle, leisure class, as on the Indian Reservations—At Malki, each Indian is to make or furnish her own pillow—& I shall add the bobbins also—I think I am teaching dependence to do otherwise—To them the Government is an unfailing source of supply, no matter how careless & indifferent they are—We are not doing justly by them, when we encourage such irresponsibility.[34]

In March of 1916, Sterling wrote from the Morongo Reservation in Banning pressing McCormick to remind Salvadora Valenzuela—the Pala woman who later that year demonstrated lace making at the Riverside County Fair—to send her "all the lace that is ready to deliver" and "a list of the names & price attached to each piece, [so] we can measure it up & send the money in checks to each worker, at once."[35] She added:

> I wrote to Salvadora last week, but she probably did not understand it—at any rate she has not attended to it—As soon as I can get it, I have to prepare it for sale & we need more at Redlands & at Riverside to meet the demand while the tourist season is on—If you will kindly see that Salvadora attends to this at once, I shall be greatly obliged.

McCormick spoke with Salvadora, who informed him that she had already written Sterling. She had four pieces of lace to send and expected more within a few days, but would send the four at once if Sterling wished it. McCormick wrote, "you [Sterling] wished her [Valenzuela] to have some other patterns made but says she cannot make the patterns you wish and will have to wait till Mrs. Lawrence returns."[36] This interaction makes clear that Mrs. Sterling wanted what she wanted when she wanted it, and was used to getting it, whether or not there was any real urgency. In addition, it suggests that there was some triangulation going on in the relationship between Sterling, Lawrence, and the Mission Indian lace makers.

All hell broke loose following Sterling's March 16 letter to McCormick. On April 4, she wrote an extraordinary letter to BIA Commissioner Sells in response to some kind of blow-up with Ellen Lawrence. She opened her letter by informing Sells that for reasons of health "and certain unexpected conditions," she intended to take a leave of at least six months from supervision of Indian lace making at Pala and Soboba, adding "I am not mentioning Morongo (or Malki) because although, over six weeks of most determined and laborious effort has been made to commence and organize the work there, by my own constant presence and also by insisting on Mrs. Lawrence (the teacher) staying there against her wishes, it cannot yet be called a success."[37] Sterling blamed this failure partly on the fact that working in the fields during the planting season kept the lace makers from their handicraft, but more forcefully on "the surprising attitude of Mrs. Lawrence herself":

> In the first place, assuming a superiority to all orders and control, and in the second place, an entire failure to assume any responsibility in regard to it; an attitude of perfect indifference and passivity toward any attempt to organize or systematize the workers into a whole—in fact, absolute inaction—letting day after day pass without making a plan, selecting patterns, or doing anything except letting the days pass—no grasp of the situation or sense of the responsibility devolving upon the teacher to make the experiment a success.

Lawrence believed in her own skill and judgment. She no longer reported to Sterling and no doubt resented being treated as a subordinate by a dominant personality inclined to micromanagement. And, as a hands-on craftswoman and teacher, she was more interested in the work itself than in its administration. For all these reasons, she stood her ground.

Sterling ascribed Lawrence's attitude—which she found "childish in the extreme"—to the recent expansion of her responsibilities and pay raise:

> [I]t might seem as if her new office and increased salary had upset her common sense. Her self-conceit is unbounded—but when it came to her asserting her superiority over me, her disposition to degrade me and treat me as an inferior and as a servant, and to persist in the grossest discourtesy,—I found it a shock to my physical, as well as my mental and moral being. There is no disappointment in life like loss of trust in a personal character, to which we had attributed upright and self-respecting qualities, and there is no redemption for it.

Having unburdened herself, Sterling added that she would provide no more patterns or thread, would reclaim equipment she had already distributed, and would not pay for completed new work. She wrote, "I have no need of a Lace Teacher nor any employment for one"—an irrelevancy at this point, since Lawrence was now fully under BIA direction, even though coordinating with Sterling. Sterling concluded with a postscript stating that when she picked up her work again in the fall, whether she would do so with Lawrence as a teacher essentially depended on Lawrence's submission. She took a parting shot at the lace teacher:

> My impression is that the whole cause of trouble has been that she does not understand, and is not competent to teach the higher and finer kinds of Lace-Making which I am trying to introduce and that she is trying to keep up a pretence [pretense] of knowing it to carry on a game of "bluff." But I am not to be deterred in my efforts to make the teaching of the higher and finer lace, Bruges, Malta, Honiton and Brussels, a part of the Indian education.

Strong words, particularly coming from someone who had earlier described Lawrence as "the most expert lace-maker in America."[38] Sterling's class consciousness and perception of insult led to these exaggerated claims. Perhaps awareness of failing health exacerbated them. She was eighty-one years old and lived just ten days after she wrote this dramatic letter.

If her words made any trouble for Lawrence, there is no record of it her BIA files. Cordelia Sterling died on April 14, 1916, leaving Ellen Lawrence to negotiate the complexities of the BIA without interference. She continued to carry out the duties of her job to the apparent satisfaction of those under whom she worked.

With Cordelia Sterling no longer the head of the RIA's Indian lace program, there was concern over that organization's continued investment of resources in government activities. The BIA arranged an early fall 1916 tour of multiple reservations by Ada L. Smith, Manager of the Sybil Carter Indian Lace Association in New York.[39] Ellen Lawrence traveled with Smith as the latter gathered information for a report about lace making prospects at Soboba, Malki, Martinez, Pala, Pechanga, and La Jolla. (Illness prevented Smith from visiting Campo, but in her October 24, 1916 report to Commissioner Sells, she noted that Lawrence could make the necessary observations there.) Smith closed her report with a vow to "endeavor upon my arrival in New York to give immediate attention to further detail in the development of the California work."

Subsequently, the BIA's direct relationship with the Sybil Carter Indian Lace Association in the disposition of California Indian lace is reflected in Ellen Lawrence's reports regarding her work on the various reservations.[40] Although the RIA remained involved, the New York-based association appears to have assumed the bulk of distribution and marketing for the government.

Ada Smith suggested in her 1916 report to the BIA commissioner that bobbin lace should replace filet lace as the main product at Soboba, the "certainty of a market being quite naturally the determining factor" in the willingness of the women there to make the change. Instruction in making multiple types of lace had clearly been provided up to this point. That Lawrence continued to teach and supervise the making of both filet and bobbin lace is indicated in her 1918 reports to Superintendent H. E. Wadsworth (successor to Harwood Hall at Soboba).

As late as 1918, when Escondido was added to her rotation of reservation visits, Lawrence's role as government lace teacher was still transforming. She wrote in her April 30, 1918 report to Wadsworth of opening a lace school at Escondido on April 15 at the home of Mrs. Agnes Balenzuela. Zahrah Preble closed her 1919 *Sunset* article about Lawrence, "She now has large classes of Indian women and girls in Pala, Saboba, Rincon, and Escondido."[41] And Lawrence's students continued to make money. Preble observed, "Some of her girls helped to swell the Third Liberty Loan when Pala, with only two hundred population, subscribed $8000."

But things were changing. Lace making was no longer as profitable as it had been. There had been supply-related problems. Plus, the California Indians sometimes pushed back against their lack of control over their work product. In one report, Lawrence informed Wadsworth that women were selling their handmade lace at fairs and other venues without telling her how much they took in and that girls were simply keeping the lace they made.[42]

In the summer of 1918, the BIA notified Ellen Lawrence that the position of lace teacher at Soboba was to be discontinued.[43] Since the Indian Service had no comparable job to offer her, she was asked what type of work she would like to do next, and where. She wrote the Commissioner of Indian Affairs on August 10, 1918, requesting a position as field matron in California, Arizona, or New Mexico.[44] In outlining strengths relevant to the position, she highlighted her day-in, day-out experience with "woman's work":

> I have been cook and housekeeper for many years. I understand the use of corn meal especially well as my family are very fond of the various corn breads so extensively used in the South. I am a fairly good seamstress and understand the use of commercial patterns. I also understand hand sewing. In recent years I have had a great deal of experience in caring for the sick. For the above reasons I think I could do a field matron's work.

The skills she listed were those of countless housewives at the time. In accordance with regulations, Lawrence was required to take a (noncompetitive) Civil Service field matron examination to bolster her application.[45]

She took the examination on October 1, 1918, while still at Soboba.[46] Visiting influenza patients at the height of the "Spanish flu" pandemic around this time, she herself caught a mild case of the virus but recovered quickly. She had little to keep her busy—she was teaching just a few women and answering the telephone—and was ready to move on. When Assistant Commissioner Meritt offered her a temporary transfer to the position of field matron at the Hoopa Valley Agency in Hoopa, California until the results of her field matron examination arrived, she accepted it.[47] Her pay would remain what it had been at Soboba ($720 a year).

But the position at Hoopa lasted only a short time. By February 1919, plans were in motion to abolish it, too.[48] Commissioner Sells consequently assigned Ellen Lawrence to New Mexico to take up the temporary post of field matron at the Pueblo of Jemez. She reported for duty in March.[49] When the results of her Civil Service examination came out in April (she received a rating of 84.15), she was permanently appointed to the job.[50]

During her years in California, Ellen Lawrence learned a great deal about the challenges of working for the BIA. Having gotten her foot in the proverbial door, she experienced first-hand the personal impact of tenuous funding, ever-evolving job responsibilities, rotating administrators, layers of bureaucracy, and a top-down agenda buffeted by shifting political and economic winds. Through her difficulties with Cordelia Sterling, she was exposed to the infighting that insinuates itself into working situations where there is competition for position or authority—a problem that would recur during Lawrence's career with the BIA.

And yet, she chose to remain in the Indian Service even though the BIA could not then offer her a position teaching her handicraft specialty. The fact that she could expect continuing employment as a result of her work in California certainly provided practical motive to stay with the agency. But there was more than that behind her decision. She had developed a connection with the Indians she encountered on a regular basis. Her upbringing may or may not have predisposed her to sympathy with Native Americans, but face-to-face interaction over time had fostered it. In writing Cato Sells on August 10, 1918 to request a field matron position, Ellen Lawrence commented, "I have enjoyed my work with the Indians so much that I should like to continue in the Service."[51] Zahrah Preble picked up on this sense of rapport, remarking that Lawrence "became vitally interested in the gentle, swift-fingered, dark-eyed Indians. At last she had found her true mission in life."[52]

Reciprocally, the Mission Indians she worked with in California valued what Ellen Lawrence could teach them. Harwood Hall's early assessment of Lawrence as matter-of-fact—someone who "just 'saws wood'"—would seem to suggest that her appeal to these Native women was based on something other than personal magnetism.[53] In May 1916, Superintendent McCormick at Pala had written Harwood Hall in Soboba to find out when Lawrence would return to Pala to teach: "The Indian Women here are asking me if she is to return, they seem to be willing to…continue the lace work if Mrs. Lawrence will teach them."[54] The mutual regard between Ellen Lawrence and her lace students in southern California reflected a shared interest in handicraft, a two-way respect for competence, and an embrace of the teaching and learning process.

Pueblo Indians were learning lace making in New Mexico simultaneously with Ellen Lawrence's teaching the craft in California, but she was sent to Jemez to take up other responsibilities.[55] Nevertheless, as her life in New Mexico unfolded, she seized an unanticipated opportunity to learn skills that, unlike lace making, both engaged her love of handicraft and, at the same time, organically represented Native culture and traditions. It proved to be a period of mid-life discovery and growth for her, one in which she stepped beyond the bounds of her own heritage.

NOTES

1. Reel, *Course of Study*, 54.

2. United States, Department of the Interior, Bureau of Indian Affairs, Commissioner of Indian Affairs Cato Sells, "Lace Making," *Annual Report of the Commissioner of Indian Affairs, for the Year 1914* (Washington: Government Printing Office, [1915]), 35.

3. Robert Fay Schrader, *The Indian Arts & Crafts Board: An Aspect of New Deal Indian Policy* (Albuquerque: University of New Mexico Press, 1983), 4.

4. Kate C. Duncan, "American Indian Lace Making," *American Indian Art Magazine*, Vol. 5, No. 3 (Summer 1980), 35, 80.

5. Deborah Dozier, "Lace Making in Southern California," *Publications by Deborah Dozier*, https://www2.palomar.edu/users/ddozier/personal_pages/publications/lace_making_in_southern_californ.htm (accessed Aug. 8, 2022).

6. Valerie Sherer Mathes, "The Redlands Indian Association: The WNIA in Southern California," *The Women's National Indian Association: A History* (Albuquerque: University of New Mexico Press, 2015), 192.

7. Sybil Carter, [remarks on lace making], "Reports from the Field," *Proceedings of the Eighth Annual Meeting of the Lake Mohonk Conference of Friends of the Indian* (Philadelphia: The Lake Mohonk Conference, 1890), 47.

8. Preble, [biographical sketch of Ellen Lawrence]; United States, Department of the Interior, Bureau of Indian Affairs, Commissioner of Indian Affairs Cato Sells, "Lace Making," *Annual Report of the Commissioner of Indian Affairs to the Secretary of the Interior for the Fiscal Year Ended June 30, 1915* (Washington: Government Printing Office, [1916]), 12.

9. Redlands Indian Association, manuscript minute book, 1904-1928, minutes for Nov. 26, 1912 meeting, 73; regarding La Casada: "Redlands Woman Dies," *Los Angeles Times*, Apr. 16, 1916, 13.

10. Commissioner of Indian Affairs Cato Sells, typed letter, signed, Washington, DC, Oct. 5, 1915, to Superintendent Thomas F. McCormick, Pala School, United States, Department of the Interior, Bureau of Indian Affairs, Record Group 75, Pala Superintendency, Correspondence, 1903-1921, Mrs. Edla Osterberg [Lacemaking], 1914-1915, Box 18, Folder 1031, National Archives, Riverside.

11. "Indian Lace Makers," *California Outlook*, Vol. 17, No. 3 (July 18, 1914), 17-18.

12. "Lace Making," BIA Commissioner *Annual Report*, 1915.

13. "Indian Lace Makers," 17.

14. Ibid.

15. Redlands Indian Association, manuscript minute book, 1904-1928, minutes for Dec. 18, 1912 meeting, 74.

16. Redlands Indian Association, manuscript minute book, 1904-1928, minutes for Apr. 26, 1913 meeting, 79.

17. Redlands Indian Association, manuscript minute book, 1904-1928, minutes for Nov. 3, 1913 meeting, 83.

18. Redlands Indian Association, manuscript minute book, 1904-1928, minutes for Dec. 10, 1913 meeting, 84.

19. BIA personnel records, Ellen Lawrence, completed personal record blank, June 7, 1915.

20. "Teaching Indians Lace Making," "In and Out of the Service [column]," *Indian School Journal*, Vol. 14, No. 8 (Apr. 1914), 382.

21. BIA personnel records, Superintendent Harwood Hall, Soboba Agency (Soboba Indian School, San Jacinto), typed letter (copy), Nov. 10, 1914, to "The Commissioner of Indian Affairs" [Cato Sells] (Washington, DC); regarding the reservations under the Soboba Agency—"Superintendents' Districts in California," "Agency and School News [column]," *Indian School Journal*, Vol. 14, No. 2 (Oct. 1913), 69.

22. BIA personnel records, "Names Certified by the Civil Service Commission for Filling the Vacancy of Lace Maker at $600.00 a Year at the Soboba School, California," typed memo, undated [Apr. or May 1915]; BIA personnel records, Emma K. Burleson, autograph letter, signed, Austin, Texas, Mar. 12, 1915, to Cato Sells (Washington, DC).

23. Superintendent Harwood Hall, Soboba Agency (Soboba Indian School, San Jacinto), typed letter, signed, Oct. 14, 1915, to Superintendent Thomas F. McCormick, Pala School (Pala), United States, Department of the Interior, Bureau of Indian Affairs, Record Group 75, Pala Superintendency, Correspondence, 1903-1921, Mrs. Edla Osterberg [Lacemaking], 1914-1915, Box 18, Folder 1031, National Archives, Riverside.

24. Commissioner of Indian Affairs Cato Sells, typed letter (copy), signature stamped, [Washington, DC], Nov. 15, 1915 (date stamped), to Superintendent Harwood Hall, Soboba School, United States, Department of the Interior, Bureau of Indian Affairs, Record Group 75, Pala Superintendency, Correspondence, 1903-1921, Mrs. Edla Osterberg [Lacemaking], 1914-1915, Box 18, Folder 1031, National Archives, Riverside.

25. Commissioner of Indian Affairs Cato Sells, typed letter (copy), signature stamped, [Washington, DC], Nov. 15, 1915 (date stamped), to Superintendent Harwood Hall, Soboba School, United States, Department of the Interior, Bureau of Indian Affairs, Record Group 75, Pala Superintendency, Correspondence, 1903-1921, Mrs. Edla Osterberg [Lacemaking], 1914-1915, Box 18, Folder 1031, National Archives, Riverside.

26. BIA personnel records, Commissioner of Indian Affairs Cato Sells, typed letter (copy), signature stamped, [Washington, DC], Dec. 10, 1915 (date stamped), to Ellen Lawrence, Soboba School.

27. Cordelia Sterling, manuscript letter, signed, on La Casa Loma letterhead,

Redlands, Dec. 16, 1915, to Superintendent Thomas F. McCormick [Pala School, (Pala)], United States, Department of the Interior, Bureau of Indian Affairs, Record Group 75, Pala Superintendency, Correspondence, 1903-1921, Lace Industry, 1914-1916, Box 14, Folder 58, National Archives, Riverside.

28. Superintendent Thomas F. McCormick, Pala School (Pala), typed letter (copy), Oct. 18, 1915, to Commissioner Cato Sells (Washington, DC), United States, Department of the Interior, Bureau of Indian Affairs, Record Group 75, Pala Superintendency, Correspondence, 1903-1921, Mrs. Edla Osterberg [Lacemaking], 1914-1915, Box 18, Folder 1031, National Archives, Riverside.

29. A June 7, 1915 personal record in Ellen Lawrence's BIA personnel files shows that she required housing for one child, age fifteen; the younger Henry Harrison Lawrence's World War I draft registration card on *Ancestry* shows him still living in Riverside County, California, in 1917-1918.

30. "Indian Institute at Sherman," *The Native American. Devoted to Indian Education*, Vol. 15, No. 28 (Sept. 5, 1914), 374-375.

31. BIA personnel records, Commissioner of Indian Affairs Cato Sells, [Washington, DC], typed letter (copy), signature stamped, June 10, 1916 (date stamped), to Ellen Lawrence, Soboba School.

32. "Sherman Institute, California," *Indian Leader. Devoted to the Interests of the American Indian*, Vol. 20, No. 4 (Sept. 29, 1916), 15.

33. "Two Indian Workers Attract Attention. Basketry and Lace Making in the Woman's Building Is a Very Entertaining Feature of Indian Day at the Fair Grounds," *Riverside Daily Press*, Vol. 31, No. 244 (Oct. 12, 1916), 3.

34. Cordelia Sterling, manuscript letter, signed, on La Casa Loma letterhead, Redlands, Dec. 16, 1915, to Superintendent Thomas F. McCormick [Pala School, (Pala)], United States, Department of the Interior, Bureau of Indian Affairs, Record Group 75, Pala Superintendency, Correspondence, 1903-1921, Lace Industry, 1914-1916, Box 14, Folder 58, National Archives, Riverside.

35. Cordelia Sterling, manuscript letter, signed, Morongo Reservation

(Banning), Mar. 14, 1916, to Superintendent Thomas F. McCormack ([Pala School, (Pala)], United States, Department of the Interior, Bureau of Indian Affairs, Record Group 75, Pala Superintendency, Correspondence, 1903-1921, Lace Industry, 1914-1916, Box 14, Folder 58, National Archives, Riverside.

36. Superintendent Thomas F. McCormick, typed letter (copy), Pala Indian School, Mar. 17, 1916, to Cordelia Sterling (Banning), United States, Department of the Interior, Bureau of Indian Affairs, Record Group 75, Pala Superintendency, Correspondence, 1903-1921, Lace Industry, 1914-1916, Box 14, Folder 58, National Archives, Riverside.

37. BIA personnel records, Cordelia Sterling, typed letter, signed, Redlands, Apr. 4, 1916, to Commissioner of Indian Affairs Cato Sells, Washington, DC.

38. BIA personnel records, as quoted in typed memorandum to "Education Employees," Nov. 25, 1914.

39. Ellen Lawrence, manuscript letter, signed, San Jacinto, Sept. 27, 1916, to Superintendent Thomas F. McCormick, Pala School (Pala), United States, Department of the Interior, Bureau of Indian Affairs, Record Group 75, Pala Superintendency, Correspondence, 1903-1921, Lace Industry, 1914-1916, Box 14, Folder 58, National Archives, Riverside; Ada L. Smith, typed letter (photostat) containing report of visit to reservations, signed, Los Angeles, Oct. 24, 1916, to "The Commissioner of Indian Affairs [Cato Sells]," Washington, DC, United States, Department of the Interior, Bureau of Indian Affairs, Record Group 75, Pala Superintendency, Correspondence, 1903-1921, Lace Industry, 1914-1916, Box 14, Folder 58, National Archives, Riverside.

40. Ellen Lawrence, three manuscript letters containing reports on lace making at southern California reservations, signed, Rincon and San Jacinto, Mar. 31, Apr. 30, and July 31, 1918, to Superintendent H. E. Wadsworth, Soboba Agency (San Jacinto), United States, Department of the Interior, Bureau of Indian Affairs, Record Group 75, Soboba Superintendency, Correspondence, 1907-1920, Lace Making Class, 1918-1918, Box 8, National Archives, Riverside.

41. Preble, [biographical sketch of Ellen Lawrence].

42. The contents of the report are characterized in Dozier, "Lace Making in Southern California."

43. BIA personnel records, Assistant Commissioner E. B. Meritt, [Washington, DC], typed letter (copy), Aug. 10, 1918 (date stamped), to Ellen Lawrence, Soboba School (San Jacinto).

44. BIA personnel records, Ellen Lawrence, [Soboba Indian School] (San Jacinto), manuscript letter, signed, Aug. 10, 1918, to "Hon. Commissioner of Indian Affairs" [Cato Sells], Washington, DC.

45. BIA personnel records, Assistant Commissioner E. B. Meritt, [Washington, DC], typed letter (copy; signature stamped), Aug. 10, 1918 (date stamped), to Ellen Lawrence, Soboba School (San Jacinto).

46. BIA personnel records, Ellen Lawrence, [Soboba Indian School] (San Jacinto), manuscript letter, signed, Oct. 31, 1918, to Superintendent H. E. Wadsworth, Soboba Agency (San Jacinto).

47. BIA personnel records, Assistant Commissioner E. B. Meritt (signature stamped), [Washington, DC], typed letter (copy), Nov. 12, 1918 (date stamped), to Ellen Lawrence, Soboba School (San Jacinto); BIA personnel records, Ellen Lawrence, [Soboba Indian School] (San Jacinto), manuscript letter, signed, Nov. 19, 1918, to "Hon. Commissioner of Indian Affairs" [Cato Sells], Washington, DC.

48. BIA personnel records, Commissioner Cato Sells (signature stamped), [Washington, DC], typed letter (copy), Feb. 17, 1919 (date stamped), to Ellen Lawrence, Hoopa Valley School ([Hoopa, California]).

49. BIA personnel records, Western Union telegram, "Indian Office," Washington, DC, Feb. 28, 1919 (date stamped), to [BIA agency], (Eureka, California).

50. BIA personnel records, President John Avery McIlhenny, United States Civil Service Commission, Washington, DC, typed letter, signed, Apr. 17, 1919, to "Commissioner of Indian Affairs" [Cato Sells], Washington, DC; BIA personnel records, Assistant Commissioner E. B. Meritt (signature stamped), [Washington, DC], typed letter (copy), Apr. 25, 1919, to Ellen Lawrence, "Through Supt. Pueblo Day Schools."

51. BIA personnel records, Ellen Lawrence, [Soboba Indian School] (San Jacinto), manuscript letter, signed, Aug. 10, 1918, to "Hon. Commissioner

of Indian Affairs" [Cato Sells], Washington, DC.

52. Preble, [biographical sketch of Ellen Lawrence].

53. Superintendent Harwood Hall, Soboba Agency (Soboba Indian School, San Jacinto), typed letter, signed, Oct. 14, 1915, to Superintendent Thomas F. McCormick, Pala School (Pala), United States, Department of the Interior, Bureau of Indian Affairs, Record Group 75, Pala Superintendency, Correspondence, 1903-1921, Mrs. Edla Osterberg [Lacemaking], 1914-1915, Box 18, Folder 1031, National Archives, Riverside.

54. Thomas F. McCormick, typed letter (copy), Pala Indian School, May 2, 1916, to Harwood Hall, Soboba Indian School (San Jacinto), United States, Department of the Interior, Bureau of Indian Affairs, Record Group 75, Pala Superintendency, Correspondence, 1903-1921, Lace Industry, 1914-1916, Box 14, Folder 58, National Archives, Riverside.

55. Mabel E. Brown, "Lace Making Among the Pueblo Indians," *Red Man*, Vol. 8, No. 9 (May 1916), 307-308.

4
Field Matron

The BIA began implementing a field matron program—"a woman-specific assimilation strategy"—in 1890.[1] The impetus behind this plan came during the 1880s from missionary groups pushing to send female reformers to reservations to teach Native women and children Christian values and Anglo domestic skills. The nineteenth-century perception of middle-class white women as imbued with particular moral authority, influence over home life, and capacity to "civilize" underpinned the venture.[2] The fact that white women had greater access to Indian homes than did men facilitated its implementation. Early in the 1880s, the Women's National Indian Association—which during the 1890s promoted the formation of the Redlands Indian Association, sponsor of Ellen Lawrence's first efforts as a lace teacher in California—dispatched female missionaries to work on reservations. This organization and others lobbied later in the 1880s for the appropriation of federal funding to support BIA assumption of responsibility for a government field matron program.[3]

In his 1893 annual report to the Secretary of the Interior, Commissioner of Indian Affairs Thomas Jefferson Morgan acknowledged the need for field matrons and the contributions toward meeting that need that had been "put forth by devoted missionaries of all denominations residing upon the reservations."[4] He described the responsibilities of the position:

> Their duties...cover everything connected with domestic work, sewing, care of children, nursing the sick, improvement of house and premises, organizing of societies for mental, moral, and social advancement of old and young, and in fact anything which a woman

of good judgment, quick sympathies, fertility of resource, large practical experience, abundant energy and sound health can find to do among an ignorant, superstitious, poor, and confiding people. Kindly house to house visitation, with practical lessons then and there of how to do what needs to be done, is the method employed, coupled with much hospitality and frequent gatherings in the home of the field matron, which home serves always as an object lesson, and often as a refuge.

These broadly framed responsibilities extended to gardening, sanitation, care of domestic animals, making butter, cheese, and honey, and observing the Sabbath.[5]

As the federal field matron program was put into practice, life experience and personal maturity—strength, resilience, independence, self-sufficiency, and the ability to interact effectively with others—outweighed professional expertise. In 1896, the job as it was then defined was given official Civil Service classification, solidifying domestic competence as the requisite qualification.[6] One BIA supervisor wrote that the field matron's work was predicated on the notion that "any good woman could teach some good women what all good women should know."[7] Thus, Ellen Lawrence's relatively limited education was not a hindrance in her transition to the role of field matron late in 1918. And although the BIA preferred young, single women for this work, many appointees varied in age and marital status from this ideal.[8] Lawrence was among a significant percentage of middle-aged and married or widowed field matrons.

By 1917, the year before Lawrence accepted her first assignment as a field matron, there were eighty-eight women working for the BIA in that capacity.[9] A desire to ameliorate the lives of Native people moved many to enter the program in its early, missionary-driven period. A more secular, Progressive-Era urge to improve society through activism later provided momentum.

There were real personal as well as potential societal benefits to the job.[10] Its challenges were offset by relatively robust compensation for an Indian Service position at the time.[11] Salary formed an incentive for many women who became field matrons after 1900. Between the end of World War I and the phasing out of the program in the 1930s (the period during which Ellen Lawrence worked as a BIA field matron), "women motivated by economic gain rather than rescue dominated the field matron corps."[12] As the wage earner for the Lawrences, Ellen was undoubtedly aware of this advantage.

The role of field matron was similar to other service-oriented jobs—librarian, nurse, teacher, social worker—that were deemed appropriate for women and opened up employment possibilities for them around the turn of the twentieth century. Such professions allowed female workers to demonstrate proficiency and earn wages in traditionally feminine ways.[13] The fact that no specific training was demanded of a field matron eventually set the job apart from these other "helping" professions. Over time, a trend toward greater education for increasingly specialized work differentiated the field matron from the field nurse—the BIA position that ultimately supplanted that of field matron. The health problems that plagued Indian reservations—tuberculosis, trachoma, infant and childhood mortality, malnutrition, and epidemics of measles and whooping cough—were more effectively managed by women who had medical background than by domestically-oriented generalists.[14] This would impact Ellen Lawrence's BIA career in New Mexico.

When Lawrence arrived at Jemez early in 1919, New Mexico was still reeling from what seemed like "the hardest winter this state has ever known."[15] Weather notwithstanding, in February 1919, BIA Commissioner Cato Sells directed her to report for duty at Albuquerque, where the BIA's Southern Pueblos Agency was headquartered, and to travel from there to the Jemez Pueblo. She showed up in Albuquerque in mid-March.[16] Her salary at Jemez would remain what it had been at Hoopa—$720 yearly. Henry Harrison Lawrence took up residence with his wife at the pueblo. At nearly twenty years old, their son was by then living independently.

Administrative expectations of what one field matron might accomplish on the job tended to be realistic. Reservation life was full of problems that domestic skill, a spirit of helpfulness, and the exemplary practice of Christian values could not in and of themselves eradicate. Nevertheless, Ellen Lawrence took up her duties at Jemez and began adapting to the place.

Pueblo of Jemez from the east, circa 1925. Elsie Clews Parsons, *The Pueblo of Jemez* (1925). Reproduced courtesy of Boston Athenaeum.

Pueblo of Jemez, plaza, circa 1925. Elsie Clews Parsons, *The Pueblo of Jemez* (1925). Reproduced courtesy of Boston Athenaeum.

Jemez was one of the pueblos under the umbrella of the Southern Pueblos Agency, which also included Acoma, Laguna, Isleta, Sandia, Zia, Santa Ana, and San Felipe. Although there were a number of differences between the various cultures represented within the agency, there were many commonalities. In general, the people of the Southern Pueblos existed on small-scale farming, maintaining sheep and goats, and taking some work for hire. They relied heavily on barter rather than cash in making purchases. Internal matters were managed by the government of each pueblo, dealings with the wider world by the agency superintendent.[17]

At Jemez, BIA staff consisted of a farmer and a field matron.[18] The school at Jemez was run by the Catholic Church. Presbyterian missionaries had set up a school there in the 1870s, but enrollment was sparse, since the Catholics among the Pueblos preferred to send their children to the Catholic mission school. The federal government began operating a school at the pueblo in the late 1890s; this merged with the Catholic school in 1909.[19]

In 1919, Leo Crane, Supervisor of the Southern Pueblos Agency, was—like Ellen Lawrence—new to his job. In his June 1920 evaluation of her, he was tentative about accurately observing and assessing from fifty-plus miles away a subordinate he hardly knew: "Insofar as any Field matron would be likely to influence the Jemez Indians, who are quite some distance removed from the Agency...Mrs. Lawrence would seem to do good work."[20]

The following February, he was more familiar with Lawrence and better prepared to evaluate her job performance, commenting that despite the isolation of the Jemez Pueblo, the conservatism of its people, and the inadequacy of the quarters there, "this field matron is doing as good work as may be expected."[21] Four months later, he relied on a source—the doctor who in tandem with Lawrence cared for Native patients at the pueblo—for first-hand information about her: "The physician who visits the pueblo finds an able assistant in this employee."[22] In November 1922, H. P. Marble (Crane's successor) was confident enough in what he knew of Lawrence to write, "seems reasonably popular with this somewhat reactionary pueblo."[23] During her first few years at Jemez, Ellen Lawrence received ratings of "good," "good-plus," or "excellent" in all of the individual performance areas the agency superintendent in Albuquerque was obliged to rank.

Infant mortality was an aspect of her job in which Lawrence made a difference at Jemez. Her 1965 obituary in the *Santa Fe New Mexican* makes clear that she took this aspect of her work seriously:

> One of her accomplishments of which she was proud is that in her six and one half years at Jemez Pueblo from 1919 to 1926 she was able, with the advice and assistance of other Indian Service personnel [personnel] to double the percentage of Indian babies to survive the first year of life. This formed an entering wedge for later...personnel to double prove even this figure.[24]

There is no mention of this in Lawrence's performance evaluations while serving at Jemez. The closest reference to her work with mothers and infants was H. P. Marble's general comment in his May 1, 1923 assessment that she engaged in "as much health work as the pueblos will receive."²⁵ Prioritizing management efficiency over sense of mission, the male administrators took this achievement of their boots-on-the-ground female employee for granted. It must sometimes have been discouraging for Lawrence to work with little guidance, peer interaction, and acknowledgment of her day-to-day work. Her isolation at Jemez forced self-direction.

In her history of the Albuquerque Indian School, Lillie McKinney provided some insight into how Ellen Lawrence gained the trust of Pueblo mothers whose first instinct was not necessarily to adopt the child care advice of a white field matron over their own ways:

> In 1919 she was transferred to Jemez, New Mexico, as field matron. The job was such a hopeless one that Mrs. Lawrence started belt weaving first, then embroidery, to save herself from "boredom." The Jemez women did not believe that a white woman could learn their embroidery, and when she succeeded their admiration for her grew so much that they permitted her to teach them how to care for their babies.²⁶

McKinney connected Lawrence's facility in learning Pueblo belt weaving and embroidery with the respect accorded her by the Native women at Jemez and with her effectiveness as a teacher of child care skills. These women were not inclined to submit to white practices until the would-be teacher had proven herself a willing and able student of something valued in their own culture—their traditional handicrafts. Lawrence and her Native students alike were simultaneously teachers and learners, which created a balance of sorts in their relationship.

Given the broad range of problems that field matrons typically faced, McKinney's assertion that Lawrence picked up belt weaving and embroidery at Jemez to escape boredom seems off the mark. Loneliness may well have plagued Ellen Lawrence at Jemez (her 1922 letter inviting her niece Mildred to visit suggests as much), but boredom was unlikely to have presented itself in a situation rife with challenges.

Ellen Lawrence cultivated an interest that she shared with the Pueblo women, deferring to their superior knowledge in mastering it. The interaction represented a two-way bridge between cultures. In seizing an opportunity to engage in handicraft, she nurtured the kind of reciprocity required to gain the confidence of the Jemez Indians. Terri Theisen has written of another, earlier, female BIA employee who lived and worked among Native Americans, "It was essential to the acculturation process that she find acceptance among those she was trying to transform."[27] Lawrence understood this dynamic. Pueblo handicrafts offered a means of entry into the lives of the women and children she was charged with helping. Eventually, Lawrence would take what the Jemez Pueblos had taught her and would teach it to other Native Americans, expanding the scope of the initial exchange.

To some extent, this transculturation process between Ellen Lawrence and the women of Jemez was a natural consequence of the intimate, sustained association of field matron and Indians:

> Imbedded in the rhetoric of...policy makers and activists was the belief that the process of assimilation was unilateral. Under the direction of Indian Service field employees, American Indians would restructure their worlds according to an Anglo-American model of life. Secure in their own sense of cultural superiority, few officials apparently ever considered it possible that cross-cultural contact might bring these women...to an assimilation experience of their own...Within the framework of "civilization" and domestic education,...bureaucrats intended that the field matrons would build an infrastructure of personal ties that would increase their efficacy as agents of cultural change...Immersion in Indian communities fostered friendships and built loyalties that brought some field matrons to different perspectives about themselves and tribal life. OIA [Office of Indian Affairs] professional standards unwittingly

made them likely candidates for the Anglo-American parallel of an Indian assimilation experience.[28]

Ellen Lawrence's career in the Indian Service provides a clear, strong example of this pattern of mutual influence.

Did Lawrence form personal connections with Native American women at Jemez? There is no evidence either to prove or disprove that she befriended any of the Pueblos on a peer basis. Considering the attitudes of the time (both Anglo and Pueblo), it would have been unusual for her to do so. But through handicraft she forged bonds that were valued long after she left Jemez. She made a positive, lasting, and documented impression on at least one young girl who, decades later, remembered Lawrence as an early mentor.

Born at the Pueblo of Jemez in 1916, Lucy Yepa was just three years old when Ellen Lawrence became the field matron there, nine when Lawrence departed for the San Felipe Pueblo in 1925. Lawrence was thus at Jemez during a formative period for Yepa. In the 1930s, Yepa attended the Albuquerque Indian School, where Lawrence then taught weaving and Pueblo embroidery. When Lawrence retired in 1936, Yepa took her place at the AIS. She studied art and handicrafts at the University of New Mexico and also taught at the Santa Fe Indian School and the Institute of American Indian Art in Santa Fe.[29] Yepa married and raised a family with Joseph Lowden, an Acoma Pueblo whom she met at the AIS.

Lucy Yepa Lowden achieved prominence as a New Mexican Native artist. A weaver, embroiderer, yucca basket maker, painter, seamstress, and poet, she is remembered in particular for her authentically rendered miniature figures of Native Americans—her "little people"—which were intended both as a "way of preserving her own Jemez heritage, as well as other Indian cultures" and "to give non-Native people a visual reference for Indian culture."[30] Some of these representations captured dancing Natives she remembered from her childhood. All were painstakingly fabricated:

These famous miniatures are about a foot high, and authentic in every detail. From her secret clay compound, which took years of experimenting to perfect, Lucy was able to reproduce the faces of the family members that influenced her life…all give off a strong sense of movement, as if they had been stopped in the midst of their activities. She…collects furs, feathers, and jewelry for her miniature friends to wear. She makes heishi [small beads of shell or stone] out of turquoise and coral, trims feathers to size, weaves tiny main sashes and kilts for the dancers, makes moccasins, and generally spares no detail for the figures. It is no wonder that they are valued and collected all over the world. Today twenty-one of her "little people" are owned by the Laboratory of Anthropology in Santa Fe…[31]

In 1987, the New Mexico Commission on the Status of Women honored Lowden on Women's Day at the New Mexico State Fair.[32] She won awards at the Santa Fe Indian Market and the Eight Northern Pueblos Arts and Crafts Show and from the Heard Museum in Phoenix (2000), as well as ribbons from numerous state and national fairs and contests. In 2005, the year she died, she was a recipient of the Southwestern Association for Indian Arts Lifetime Achievement award.

In her seventies, Lowden remembered Ellen Lawrence at Jemez. A writer for the *Santa Fe New Mexican* reported, "While Lowden follows pueblo tradition in her weaving and embroidery, she credits an Anglo nurse [that is, field matron] from the Ozarks, who worked at Jemez Pueblo."[33] Lowden recalled "Pueblo women weaving when she was a child, although she says she was too young to value their work."[34] She noted that Lawrence "had the skills in her background and started copying some of those designs…I was a young thing. She liked me. I wasn't very interested at the time. But she taught me."[35]

Lowden perceived that Lawrence was both teacher and student of the Jemez women. She commented that she herself learned her people's weaving and embroidery from the Anglo woman, who in turn had learned "this ancient craft" while at the pueblo.³⁶

As Lucy's teacher at the AIS in the 1930s, Lawrence was determined that the young woman fully develop her gifts. Joe Sando wrote:

> As a teenager at the Albuquerque Indian School in the early 1930s, Lucy was [formally] introduced to weaving and embroidery by Mrs. Ellen Lawrence, who had learned the pueblo's ancient art at Jemez when she was a field nurse [matron] living at the old Presbyterian Mission grounds. At first Lucy did not really enjoy crafts, but Mrs. Lawrence almost literally pushed her into them; they later proved to be a stepping stone to greater things for Lucy.³⁷

Lawrence's experience with Lucy Yepa was not unique. An effective teacher, she also sparked a lasting interest in Pueblo textile handicrafts among AIS students who went on to produce prized woven goods for the Tewa Weaving Industry store in Isleta.³⁸

Superintendent Marble was aware of Lawrence's attention to Native crafts. In his November 1, 1922 efficiency report on her, he commented, "Manifests much interest in native crafts and arts."³⁹ Six months later, on May 1, 1923, he wrote, "Very much interested in native crafts and arts; does much to encourage same."⁴⁰ A well-known visitor to the Pueblo at Jemez in 1921 and 1922 also made note of Lawrence's engagement with Native handicrafts.

Sociologist, anthropologist, folklorist, and feminist Elsie Clews Parsons (1875-1941) conducted extensive field research among the Pueblos and other Native tribes of the southwest in the first half of the twentieth century. She wrote scholarly works about their cultures at a time when few systematic studies on the subject were available. Based on years of direct observation of Pueblo life, her influential *Pueblo Indian Religion* was published in 1939. In 1921 and 1922, while Lawrence was working at Jemez, Parsons was concurrently carrying out field work there "as part of a general ethnological survey...among the Pueblos of Arizona and New Mexico."[41] Her observations appeared in 1925 under the title *The Pueblo of Jemez*.

In that volume, Parsons covered handicrafts at Jemez in a paragraph beginning, "Local handicraft is meagre."[42] She touched briefly on pottery, fire stones for baking paper (wafer) bread, and basketry, then turned to weaving: "There is no cloth weaving, but recently the matron of the Indian Service has set up in her house looms for weaving blankets and belts, and several girls are taking up the work. It will be interesting to see whether the innovation of weaving by women, instead of by men, will 'take'."[43] Parsons concluded with a few sentences on moccasins, beads, dance bandoliers, masks, tablitas (ceremonial headdresses), and prayer-sticks.[44]

Charles Lummis, photographer. Pueblo woman weaving belt on a belt loom, 1889. Library of Congress collections.

This snapshot of Lawrence's efforts to revive the art of weaving at Jemez is tantalizing. It does not reveal whether she used a Native upright (vertical) loom for fabric or whether she used a European-style horizontal loom, nor whether she employed a Pueblo backstrap loom for making narrower items like belts and sashes. (The backstrap loom involved the weaver sitting on the floor or ground with legs stretched out in front, one of the two rods holding the warp threads attached to a strap around the weaver's waist, the loom resting in the weaver's lap.) The use of a non-Pueblo loom or looms would have equated to adaptation rather than preservation.

While Parsons insinuated that women practicing what had traditionally been a male handicraft might generate some resistance, Lucy Yepa Lowden's late-life recall of Pueblo women weaving when she was a child implies that Lawrence met with some success in encouraging women weavers at Jemez.

In the newsletter *Indians at Work* in the 1930s, Edith Nash—wife of Philleo Nash, Commissioner of Indian Affairs from 1961 to 1966, under Presidents John Kennedy and Lyndon Johnson—vividly described the Pueblo embroidery she saw while doing field studies among the Zuni people. In color, design, and technique, this embroidery shared much with that of Jemez. Nash wrote:

> We had seen...such embroideries, that we were left with an overwhelming sense of the magnitude of design sealed in the centuries of this people's past. Designs of so sacred a nature their conception had been made in the secrecy of the Kiva—that ceremonial chamber where the men in early times did the weaving and embroidering.

> The embroidery of the Pueblo Indians is sacred to their ceremonies. Highly conventionalized, dynamically abstract, it survived four hundred years of Spanish invasion. In no instance does it become florid. Practically always it follows the geometric terraces of mountains and clouds...

> On cotton dance kilts and mantas Pueblo embroidery nearly always takes the form of a broad band of black wool with two vertical stripes of green appearing at intervals. On these broad borders the only space not completely covered is a thin meandering line of the white cotton base which appears diagonally crossing the black and green. This white design line creates a strong off-balance movement to the general vertical embroidery, seeming to exaggerate the movement of the dance in which it is used.
>
> Set in these terraced borders are frequently [seen] medallions of special significance and strong color, red or green usually. Symbolically, we are told, vertical red is rain, and green the color of fertility.[45]

She noted, too, that the stitches on a manta or dance kilt were worked by counting threads rather than from a drawn pattern—"How tireless is the counting of the threads as she [the Zuni embroiderer] works to make her involved geometric patterns come out evenly!"[46] Regarding weaving, Nash quoted a Hopi trader, who remarked to her, "They don't weave much, anymore."[47] Nash's BIA newsletter article bespeaks the growing attention to Native textile crafts taking hold within the agency as Ellen Lawrence was striving to master Pueblo embroidery and weaving—a trend that continued into the 1930s and flourished in an administrative atmosphere that affirmed it.

The form used to assess employee performance while Ellen Lawrence worked for the BIA included sections for identifying books and periodicals read by the evaluee over the previous year. Presumably reported by the supervised to the supervisor, this information would have provided some measure of employee motivation to build knowledge related to the position held. Lawrence's efficiency reports while at Jemez and, subsequently, at San Felipe only intermittently contain listings of her reading. Nevertheless, those that do are revealing. They show her selecting reading matter in response to both the explicit demands of her job and, simultaneously, to her personal passion for handicraft, essentially reshaping the position to synthesize work and self.

In his November 1, 1924 report on her, Chester Faris—Special Supervisor in Charge of the Southern Pueblos Agency—listed under "Books read during past twelve months" *Zuñi Weaving Technique* by Leslie Spier (a specialized title published in 1924 in the journal *American Anthropologist*) and, under "Periodicals for which employee is a regular subscriber," the popular *Modern Priscilla*, to which Lawrence herself had contributed.[48] These writings represented, respectively, the arcane Native craft traditions Lawrence was then learning and the range of Anglo domestic crafts which the BIA deemed suitable for acculturating Indian women. (The periodical listing also includes the *Saturday Evening Post* and *Albuquerque Journal*, indicating that Lawrence paid some attention to the world beyond the pueblo.)

In his May 1, 1925 assessment of Lawrence, Superintendent Loson L. Odle enumerated a longer list of books read—*Infant Care, Child Care and Child Welfare, Health of the Family* (the authors of these first three titles unidentified), *The Care and Feeding of Children* by L. Emmett Holt, Speir's *Zuñi Weaving Technique* (listed again), and "several books of fiction."[49] The periodicals itemized included *The Modern Priscilla, Needle Craft*, the popular *American Magazine* and *Saturday Evening Post*, and "two daily newspapers." Lawrence may have taken pains to ensure that this new superintendent was apprised of the scope of what she had read and its relevance to her ongoing work, or perhaps Loson made proactive inquiries about the employees under his direction.

As Lawrence endeavored to bring job performance and personal fulfillment closer together, she faced obstacles that distracted her from both.

The fact that Jemez was anything but a population center made it necessary for her to travel to Albuquerque to manage ordinary details of her life. In January 1924, she wrote Superintendent Marble at the Southern Pueblos

Agency for permission to leave Jemez to visit a dentist in Albuquerque for fillings.[50] Obtaining permission took time, and travel to Albuquerque pulled her away from her job, her declining husband, and her handiwork.

Moreover, an unsettling attempt by a Catholic priest at the Pueblo of Jemez to supplant Lawrence with another field matron endangered her good standing as a BIA employee in 1924. On June 9 of that year, the Reverend Sixtus Kopp sent a letter from the pueblo to Andrieus (Andrew) A. Jones, Democratic United States senator from New Mexico, requesting that Lawrence be transferred and replaced by Miss Anna Siebert from Dulce, New Mexico, where the Jicarilla Apache reservation was located. He elaborated, "This Mrs. Lawrence here is not liked by these Indians and is causing more or less trouble, while if sent to Dulce she would be with more of her own kind; on the other hand I feel confident that Miss Siebert would welcome the change to the Jemes Pueblo."[51] The meaning of the phrase "where she would be with more of her own kind" is uncertain, but it was clearly intended to be derogatory.

Senator Jones forwarded the letter to BIA Commissioner Burke, who sent a copy to Chester Faris asking for insight into the "inharmonious conditions existing in the Jemes Pueblo."[52] Faris visited Jemez on June 19 to talk with Pueblo Indians, BIA employees, and Ellen Lawrence herself. He reported to Commissioner Burke:

> During the day I heard nothing against Mrs. Lawrence and too little in her favor. All reports in this office are much in her favor but I did take occasion to call her attention to the form and brevity of her regular weekly reports...She has been at the Pueblo for some years and in my short acquaintance with her work it would be unfair to recommend her transfer. However, if it is thought advisable...I should dislike to see Miss Anna Siebert [replace Lawrence]...for one reason that she is no more efficient and for the additional reason that I have too often known administrative embarrassment by just such transfers. Because of her five years work with me at Dulce, she could feel and others would feel that the transfer had our support and the

atmosphere resulting in similar cases is too often unfortunate and seldom factors to the betterment of the service in general.[53]

Faris backed Ellen Lawrence against this odd and ultimately unsuccessful maneuver. There is no reference to it in her subsequent personnel evaluations. Moreover, later in 1924 her salary was increased from $720 to $1,200 annually.[54] Why had Kopp initiated the fuss? Long-standing tension between Catholics and Presbyterians at the pueblo may have been part of the story. Although the number of Presbyterians residing at Jemez was then in serious decline, Lawrence was among them, and she did, in fact, attend Presbyterian services until she left Jemez for the San Felipe Pueblo.[55] Or perhaps she had developed too much influence over the women of Jemez for Kopp's liking.

Most problematic of Lawrence's challenges, Henry Harrison Lawrence's long, slow deterioration began to hinder his wife's ability to dependably meet work expectations at Jemez and, subsequently, San Felipe. Her personnel records for 1925 and 1926 show that his condition was worsening. He required a level of care that was difficult for a woman with a full-time job to provide.

In November 1923, Superintendent Marble appraised Ellen Lawrence, "Gives good service to the Jemez pueblo. Also has care of a blind husband."[56] On May 1, 1924, Marble's temporary replacement Chester Faris commented, "An efficient employee who has an added responsibility in the care of a blind husband."[57] Faris wrote later in 1924, "Interested and strives to render good service. Care of an invalid husband adds to her responsibilities."[58] In the spring of 1925, Henry Lawrence suffered a health crisis. His wife wrote Superintendent Odle apologizing for submitting a sparse report for the week ending April 4, asking for some leave, and adding as explanation for the short notice on the requested leave, "My husband was very ill last week but is now much improved, and since Monday morning I have been doing my usual Indian work."[59] In his May 1925 evaluation, Odle observed "Good as field matrons go. Has a husband eighty-two years old who needs considerable care."[60]

By June 1925, Commissioner of Indian Affairs Charles Burke, who prioritized health and education issues on the reservations and in the pueblos, was considering ways to restructure the agency's personnel to better address them.[61] Ellen Lawrence now had to cope with growing administrative opinion that field nurses could more cost-effectively dispense the medical services sorely needed by Native Americans than could field matrons.

Having been apprised of Henry Lawrence's condition, Burke wrote Odle:

> The Office understands that the husband of Mrs. Ellen Lawrence, the present incumbent in this position, is past ninety years of age and is at present a bedridden invalid and to transfer her at this time would be inadvisable. For this reason, action regarding the abolishment of this place will be held in abeyance for the present, but the Office wishes to again express its appreciation of your cooperation in the economy program insofar as such program affects salaries and rents under your supervision.[62]

Henry Lawrence had cataract surgery at the trachoma hospital in Albuquerque around this time. Shortly thereafter, Ellen Lawrence was transferred to the Pueblo of San Felipe in Algodones, which was, like Jemez, in Sandoval County, and had about the same Native population. With Henry in tow, she took the place of Mary E. Dennis, the San Felipe field matron, who was temporarily on special duty at the trachoma hospital. The precariousness of Lawrence's position and her husband's downward spiral required fortitude, but she soldiered on. Unfortunately, Henry's condition was now squarely on the BIA radar screen, and it only got worse.

In the summer of 1924, Burke had hired public health nurse and American Red Cross employee Elinor D. Gregg to oversee the BIA's field matron and field nurse programs. She began visiting reservations to assess health conditions shortly thereafter.[63] She inspected the Southern Pueblos in New Mexico between April 27 and May 7 of the following year and summarized her findings and recommendations in a report submitted in June 1925, just before Lawrence transferred from Jemez to San Felipe.

As a skilled professional, Gregg was critical of the limited impact field matrons in general had been able to make on the health of the Pueblo Indians. She advised reorganizing the pueblos into groupings and substituting field nurses with automobile transportation for travel between multiple pueblos for field matrons tethered to a single location. She wrote:

> It should be understood that the field nurse will do some work along the lines of home-making and family social case work. The main emphasis of her endeavor will be health service, both curative treatment and health education. The public health nurse is trained for this work and her efforts should show the results of her training in her knowledge and in her methods of work.[64]

Gregg's recommendations made sense in terms of both efficiency and potential benefits to Native health. Moreover, they were in accord with Commissioner Burke's thoughts on phasing out the BIA field matron program. But they did not bode well for Ellen Lawrence's situation.

Gregg made specific observations on the circumstances at each pueblo she visited, including Jemez. Her comments on Lawrence are illuminating:

> Mrs. Lawrence was at one time lace-making teacher in the Southern California Indian Schools. Her work is almost entirely along the lines of sewing and allied arts or industries. She can spin, weave, make lace, and pick out any sort of handicraft. At present her time is encroached upon by the condition of her invalid husband. He is slowly dying of old age, is bed-ridden and can scarcely last much longer. Her value to the health service among the Indians is almost nil. Apart from her present disability on account of her husband,

her interest in health matters is of the slightest. In the presence of the Indians she speaks scornfully of their appreciation of the benefits of white man's medicine. Her remarks may all be true but it is poor policy to mention that when the doctor is trying to persuade them to take treatment.[65]

Lawrence had been miscast as a field matron. She was moved more by fascination with handicraft than by bureau mandates. Disinclined to conform wholeheartedly to the BIA program, she was something of a square peg in a round hole.

But even with her personal idiosyncrasies admitted, her defiant stance in relation to the Natives' practice of their own medicine is striking. It is not surprising that Gregg—who had expertise in medical matters—would dismiss Lawrence's untutored management of Pueblo health. But it is unexpected that an Anglo field matron would support the value of traditional Pueblo healing over white medicine. Such a stance was at the time more characteristic of Native American than white women in the field matron corps: "Indian field matrons entered the program in 1895 confident of their ability to assist other tribal women in the assimilation process...The assimilated personas these women projected in their work was not, however, totally seamless...They particularly did not try to challenge the status of native health care practitioners or ridicule those who accepted their help."[66] Lawrence had seemingly come to respect aspects of Pueblo culture through her years of living at Jemez.

Gregg undoubtedly aspired to improve Native American lives. However, in her general comments about the Pueblos she betrayed the ingrained racism of her time: "Compared with other Indians these Indians are more productive, industrious and thrifty than most. Compared with Mexicans and white people with like resources they are about on an equal plane with the Mexican and a little below the white man."[67] Lawrence may well have taken umbrage at Gregg's condescension toward the Pueblos, the more so because it was coupled with some disdain for the field matron herself.

In the wake of Gregg's visit and report, Superintendent Odle of the Southern Pueblos Agency advised Commissioner Burke in June 1925 to abolish the field matron position at Jemez. Burke agreed but recommended in his June 22 letter to Odle to hold off on doing so until Henry Lawrence's situation was resolved.[68] Since Ellen Lawrence was offered and was willing to accept the temporarily vacant field matron position at San Felipe, she had some reprieve.[69]

San Felipe Pueblo, between 1871 and 1907. NARA (College Park).

At San Felipe as at Jemez, Lawrence received positive personnel evaluations. Her rapidly-changing supervisors found her a capable worker but could not responsibly ignore the disruption to her work her husband created. On November 1, 1925, S. A. M. Young, the new Supervisor in Charge of the Southern Pueblos Agency, evaluated her: "The above is my estimate based on short acquaintance [all good, good-plus, and excellent ratings]. I believe Mrs. Lawrence is a satisfactory employee. She is hampered by a senile,

Much to Learn, Much to Give   97

helpless husband, who probably will not live very long."⁷⁰ Young's May 1, 1926 evaluation went farther regarding Henry's debility: "Mrs. Lawrence is probably doing as well as could be expected considering that she is handicapped by a very old invalid husband who is constantly expected to die but does not die, and who by reason of age has little mentality."⁷¹

The situation was not sustainable. Young was obliged to report on it to the Commissioner of Indian Affairs, along with that of the Southern Pueblos field matron at Isleta, Lenore Shafer, who also had an ailing husband.⁷² Commissioner Burke directed Young to instruct both women to find caretakers for their husbands so that they could devote their full attention to work responsibilities. He indicated that failure to do so would result in the "assignment of other field matrons or field nurses to these places." Ellen Lawrence's job security was doubly threatened.

Lawrence's first instinct was to downplay the seriousness of her husband's condition. On May 27, 1926, she wrote Young:

> In answer to yours of May 24, I wish to state first that my husband is far from helpless. He is 82 years old and has a weak heart, but he dresses himself, makes his bed, comes to the table for his meals, and goes alone to the outdoor toilet. All that I have to do for him is to prepare his three simple meals each day. In fact—he makes less demand on my time and strength than ever before in the 30 years of our married life.⁷³

She went on to explain that she had taken leave time to care for him while ill the previous year, had not "lost a day's work" since October, and that her husband's cataract surgery had restored "fair vision" to him.

However, she had no choice but to comply with supervisory directives. She added in her May 27 letter that Henry would stay with her son and daughter-in-law in Española, where he would remain "If the Commissioner wishes me to do field matron work in more than one Pueblo." Her future with the BIA was up in the air: "If I stay at San Felipe I shall send for my 18-year-old niece to stay with us here. Until she comes Mr. Lawrence stays in Española." Between her husband's infirmity and the uncertainty of her working situation, it was a difficult time.

Lawrence's plans to care for her husband did not work out as proposed to Young, however. She informed new Southern Pueblos Superintendent T. F. McCormick by letter on July 19, 1926 that her daughter-in-law had stayed with her for five weeks, but that none of her nieces was able or willing to take up residence at San Felipe. Her son's wife could not remain at Algodones indefinitely and, evidently, the idea of Henry Lawrence going home with her had been abandoned. Ellen Lawrence consequently engaged twenty-two-year-old Santana Tenorio—"the Indian girl who has been my helper since I have been in San Felipe"—to remain with Henry every day while she herself was working in the pueblo. She obviously respected Tenorio's competence:

> She is a good worker and a good housekeeper. She does all my work except the cooking, and as she takes all her meals at home I cook only for myself and Mr. Lawrence. Santana stays at her home nights, but she lives quite near me and if I should ever need her outside of her regular work-hours I can easily call her.[74]

In something of a role reversal, then, a Native American served as Ellen Lawence's social support system when her family did not rise fully to the occasion, ensuring that Henry had round-the-clock supervision while his wife fulfilled the responsibilities of her job. It was a solution that Commissioner Burke could accept.

Although there is no evidence that Ellen Lawrence was actively learning and teaching textile crafts at San Felipe, handicraft remained a vital interest—one which she was allowed to indulge in the increasingly animated Native arts community of New Mexico. The same day she wrote McCormick about Santana Tenorio's assistance with her husband, she also wrote him another letter to express gratitude for leave to work early in August at the Santa Fe Indian Fair, where Native arts and crafts were showcased: "I can only say that I am glad to go. It is <u>my</u> summer school and vacation in one. Thank you for permission to go."[75]

Ellen Lawrence carried a heavy load during this period, but she nevertheless managed to make the acquaintance of a fellow Missourian, another Anglo woman who became a close personal friend. Like Lawrence, Julia West Parker (1881-1973) was born in Texas County. A long-time Missouri resident, she was an active member of a number of local organizations and a writer about Houston (Missouri) and Texas County for newspaper and periodical publication. She spent a number of winters in Albuquerque and was a collector of Native American pottery. Lawrence's 1965 obituary in the *Houston Herald* stated that the two met in New Mexico "39 years ago"—which would have been 1926.[76] Lawrence must have treasured her association with a contemporary who shared both her regional roots and her appreciation of the Native crafts of New Mexico.

Henry Harrison Lawrence's long, slow decline had tested his wife's fortitude throughout their years at Jemez and San Felipe. On January 13, 1927, he finally passed away at the Pueblo of San Felipe at the age of eighty-three. The primary cause of his death was lobar pneumonia, with senility listed as a contributing factor.[77] He had been isolated from the outside world for so long that a full-length obituary was deemed unnecessary—only the briefest of funeral notices appeared in the *Albuquerque Journal* for January 14. He was buried in Fairview Memorial Park in Albuquerque. Although Henry and Ellen Lawrence had shared three decades together, his death could only have come as a release for her.

Ellen Lawrence was not as successful in forming the kind of connection with the San Felipe Pueblos as she had been at Jemez. Superintendent McCormick was favorably disposed toward her—he described her in his November 1, 1926 evaluation as "a conscientious hard working woman"—

but observed that she was "making very little progress with the Indians with whom she is working."[78] She may have had less opportunity at San Felipe to engage in handicrafts than she had had at Jemez. The necessity of establishing herself in a new situation and the trials she faced during her husband's final months surely interfered with the time and energy she could put into creating the give and take with the Pueblos that she had developed at Jemez.

Meanwhile, internal pressure to increase the corps of BIA field nurses stepped up decision-making regarding pueblos served by field matrons. By May 1, 1927, despite his regard for Lawrence, McCormick was ready to recommend her transfer to a boarding school where her considerable textile skills would find a better outlet. H. J. Warner (a BIA district medical director) added to McCormick's comment, "I recommend that Mrs. Ellen Lawrence be transferred to a boarding school, and the vacancy be filled with a field Nurse."[79]

Ellen Lawrence was once again compelled to start over. She was a resilient woman, but she was in her mid-fifties, had experienced a fair amount of stress, and could no longer count on unfailing stamina. Fortunately, the groundwork laid during her time at Jemez served her well in transitioning to the next stage of her life. A changing perspective from the top level of government down on the merits of preserving Native culture and traditions would dovetail with Lawrence's personal aspirations. She would at last be able to focus on the work she most wanted to do and for which she was uniquely trained, and her expertise would be recognized and celebrated, albeit not immediately.

NOTES

1. "Field Matrons," *Encyclopedia of the Great Plains*, David J. Wishart, ed., http://plainshumanities.unl.edu/encyclopedia/doc/egp.gen.013 (accessed Feb. 6, 2022).

2. Terri Christian Theisen, "'With a View Toward Their Civilization': Women and the Work of Indian Reform," master's thesis, Portland State University, 1996, 23-24, 26-28.

3. Ibid., 19-20.

4. United States, Department of the Interior, Bureau of Indian Affairs, Commissioner of Indian Affairs Thomas Jefferson Morgan, "Field Matrons," *Sixty-Second Annual Report of the Commissioner of Indian Affairs to the Secretary of the Interior. 1893* (Washington: Government Printing Office, 1893), 56.

5. Theisen, 37-38.

6. Ibid., 36, 39.

7. Elinor D. Gregg, as quoted in Sandra K. Schackel, "'The Tales Those Nurses Told!' Public Health Nurses Among the Pueblo and Navajo Indians," *New Mexico Historical Review*, Vol. 65, No. 2 (Apr. 1990), 229.

8. Lisa Emmerich, "'Right in the Midst of My Own People': Native American Women and the Field Matron Program," *American Indian Quarterly*, Vol. 15, No. 2 (Spring 1991), 203.

9. Theisen, 35.

10. Ibid., 40.

11. Emmerich, "Right in the Midst of My Own People," 204.

12. "Field Matrons," *Encyclopedia of the Great Plains*.

13. Theisen, 39.

14. "Field Matrons," *Encyclopedia of the Great Plains*.

15. "The Groundhog Comes Out," *Albuquerque Journal*, Mar. 16, 1919, 16; "Heavy Snows in Mountain Areas During February." *Albuquerque Journal*, Mar. 17, 1919, 2; "Severe Winter But No Record-Breaker, Says Weather Man," *Santa Fe New Mexican*, Mar. 27, 1919, 5.

16. BIA personnel records, Commissioner of Indian Affairs Cato Sells, [Washington, DC], typed letter, signed, Feb. 17, 1919 (date stamped), to Ellen Lawrence, Hoopa Valley School; BIA personnel records, Western

Union telegram, "Indian Office," Washington, DC, Feb. 28, 1919 (date stamped), to [BIA agency], (Eureka, California).

17. Gregg, "Report," 1, 4.

18. Ibid., 3.

19. Sando, *Nee Hemish*, 151-154.

20. BIA personnel records, Superintendent Leo Crane, Southern Pueblos Agency (Albuquerque, New Mexico), efficiency report, June 30, 1920.

21. BIA personnel records, Superintendent Leo Crane, Southern Pueblos Agency (Albuquerque, New Mexico), efficiency report, Feb. 1, 1921.

22. BIA personnel records, Superintendent Leo Crane, Southern Pueblos Agency (Albuquerque, New Mexico), efficiency report, June 30, 1921.

23. BIA personnel records, Superintendent H. P. Marble, Southern Pueblos Agency (Albuquerque, New Mexico), efficiency report, Nov. 1, 1922.

24. "Lawrence, Ellen [obituary]," *Santa Fe New Mexican*, Nov. 12, 1965, 14.

25. BIA personnel records, Superintendent H. P. Marble, Southern Pueblos Agency (Albuquerque, New Mexico), efficiency report, May 1, 1923.

26. McKinney, "History of the Albuquerque Indian School (Concluded)," footnote 58, 320.

27. Theisen, 81-82.

28. Lisa E. Emmerich, "'Civilization' and Transculturation: The Field Matron Program and Cross-Cultural Contact," *American Indian Culture and Research Journal*, Vol. 15, No. 4 (1991), 34.

29. Katherine Saltzstein, "Artist Helps Preserve Her Culture," *Albuquerque Journal*, Jan. 13, 1991, 26.

30. Sando, *Nee Hemish*, 186; Marissa Stone, "Jemez Pueblo artist Lowden dies at 89," *Santa Fe New Mexican*, May 6, 2005, B005.

31. Sando, *Nee Hemish*, 186.

32. Ibid., 187.

33. Dean Balsamo, "Lucy Yepa Lowden gives insight into world of her 'little people'," *Santa Fe New Mexican*, June 12, 1992, 72.

34. Saltzstein, "Artist Helps Preserve Her Culture."

35. Ibid.

36. Katherine Augustine, "Pair inspired others with their art and soul," *Albuquerque Tribune*, Mar. 16, 2000, 20.

37. Sando, *Nee Hemish*, 186.

38. "Isleta Weaving, Clothing, and Tanning—Part I," *Isleta Pueblo News*, Vol. 16, No. 5 (May 2021), 20.

39. BIA personnel records, Superintendent H. P. Marble, Southern Pueblos Agency (Albuquerque, New Mexico), efficiency report, Nov. 1, 1922.

40. BIA personnel records, Superintendent H. P. Marble, Southern Pueblos Agency (Albuquerque, New Mexico), efficiency report, May 1, 1923.

41. Alfred V. Kidder, "Foreword," Elsie Clews Parsons, *The Pueblo of Jemez*, Papers of the Southwestern Expedition, Number 3 (New Haven: Published by the Yale University Press for the Department of Archaeology, Phillips Academy, Andover, Massachusetts, 1925), ix.

42. Parsons, *The Pueblo of Jemez*, 16.

43. Ibid., 16-17

44. Ibid., 17.

45. Edith Nash, "Indian Embroidery," *Indians at Work: A News Sheet for Indians and the Indian Service*, Vol. 3, No. 19 (May 15, 1936), 22-23. In writing this piece, Nash consulted Lawrence on why Hopi men instead of women did all the weaving and embroidery for their people; Lawrence answered by quoting what a Hopi man had told her —see page 25 of the article.

46. Ibid., 23.

47. Ibid., 24.

48. BIA personnel records, Special Supervisor in Charge C. E. Faris, Southern Pueblos Agency (Albuquerque, New Mexico), efficiency report, Nov. 1, 1924.

49. BIA personnel records, Superintendent Loson L. Odle, Southern Pueblos Agency (Albuquerque, New Mexico), efficiency report, May 1, 1925.

50. BIA personnel records, Ellen Lawrence, autograph letter, signed, Jemez Pueblo (Jemez, New Mexico), Jan. 28, 1924, to Superintendent H. P. Marble, Southern Pueblos Agency (Albuquerque, New Mexico).

51. BIA personnel records, Reverend Sixtus Kopp, Jemez Pueblo (New Mexico), typed letter (copy), June 9, 1924, to Senator Andrew [Andrieus] Jones, United States Senate (Washington, DC).

52. BIA personnel records, Commissioner of Indian Affairs Charles H. Burke, [Washington, DC], typed letter (copy), signature stamped, June 20, 1924 (date stamped), to Special Supervisor in Charge Chester E. Faris, Southern Pueblos Agency (Albuquerque, New Mexico).

53. BIA personnel records, Special Supervisor in Charge Chester E. Faris, Southern Pueblos Agency (Albuquerque, New Mexico), typed letter, signed, June 23, 1924, to "The Commissioner of Indian Affairs" (Washington, DC).

54. BIA personnel records, Special Supervisor in Charge C. E. Faris, efficiency report, Nov. 1, 1924.

55. Sando, *Nee Hemish*, 154.

56. BIA personnel records, Superintendent H. P. Marble, Southern Pueblos Agency (Albuquerque, New Mexico), efficiency report, Nov. 1, 1923.

57. BIA personnel records, Special Supervisor in Charge C. E. Faris, efficiency report, May 1, 1924.

58. BIA personnel records, Special Supervisor in Charge C. E. Faris, efficiency report, Nov. 1, 1924.

59. BIA personnel records, Ellen Lawrence, autograph letter, signed, Jemez Pueblo (Jemez, New Mexico), Apr. 7, 1925, to Superintendent Loson L. Odle, Southern Pueblos Agency (Albuquerque, New Mexico).

60. BIA personnel records, Superintendent Loson L. Odle, Southern Pueblos Agency (Albuquerque, New Mexico), efficiency report, May 1, 1925.

61. Jacqueline S. Pflaum, "Helper Woman: A Biography of Elinor Delight Gregg," doctoral thesis, Philip Y. Hahn School of Nursing, University of San Diego, 1996, 82.

62. BIA personnel records, Commissioner of Indian Affairs Charles H. Burke, Washington, DC, typed letter, signed, June 22, 1925 (date stamped), to Superintendent Loson L. Odle, Southern Pueblos Agency (Albuquerque, New Mexico).

63. Pflaum, "Helper Woman," 107, 122.

64. Gregg, "Report," 6.

65. Ibid., 11.

66. Emmerich, "Right in the Midst of My Own People," 210-211.

67. Gregg, "Report," 4.

68. BIA personnel records, Commissioner of Indian Affairs Charles H. Burke, Washington, DC, typed letter, signed, June 22, 1925 (date stamped), to Superintendent Loson L. Odle, Southern Pueblos Agency (Albuquerque, New Mexico).

69. BIA personnel records, Superintendent Loson L. Odle, Southern Pueblos Agency (Albuquerque, New Mexico), typed letter, signed, June 30, 1925, to "The Commissioner of Indian Affairs" [Charles H. Burke], Washington, DC.

70. BIA personnel records, Supervisor in Charge S. A. M. Young, efficiency report, Nov. 1, 1925. Lawrence's excellent ratings were for "Openness to suggestion," "Adaptability," "Courtesy to others," "Manners and speech," and "Kindness to pupils."

71. BIA personnel records, Supervisor in Charge S. A. M. Young, efficiency report, May 1, 1926.

72. BIA personnel records, Commissioner of Indian Affairs Charles H. Burke, Washington, DC, typed letter, signed, May 20, 1926 (date stamped), to Supervisor in Charge S. A. M. Young, Southern Pueblos Agency (Albuquerque, New Mexico).

73. BIA personnel records, Ellen Lawrence, autograph letter, signed, San

Felipe Pueblo (Algodones, New Mexico), May 27, 1926, to Supervisor in Charge S. A. M. Young, Southern Pueblos Agency (Albuquerque, New Mexico).

74. BIA personnel records, Ellen Lawrence, autograph letter, signed, San Felipe Pueblo (Algodones, New Mexico), July 19, 1926, to Superintendent T. F. McCormick, Southern Pueblos Agency (Albuquerque, New Mexico).

75. BIA personnel records, Ellen Lawrence, autograph letter, signed, San Felipe Pueblo (Algodones, New Mexico), July 19, 1926, to Superintendent T. F. McCormick, Southern Pueblos Agency (Albuquerque, New Mexico); BIA personnel records, L. R. M. McDonald, typed letter, signed, San Ysidro, New Mexico, July 29, 1926, to Superintendent T. F. McCormick, Southern Pueblos Agency (Albuquerque, New Mexico).

76. "Ellen Ross Lawrence [obituary]," *Houston Herald* (Houston, Missouri), Dec. 2, 1965, 9; "Julia West Parker [obituary]," *Houston Herald*, Aug. 30, 1973, 4.

77. New Mexico, Bureau of Public Health, original certificate of death for Henry Harrison Lawrence, Jan. 1927, *FamilySearch*, https://ancestors.familysearch.org/en/LB44-C53/henry-harrison-lawrence-i-1843-1927 (accessed Aug. 4, 2022).

78. BIA personnel records, Superintendent T. F. McCormick, Southern Pueblos Agency (Albuquerque, New Mexico), efficiency report, Nov. 1, 1926

79. BIA personnel records, Superintendent T. F. McCormick, Southern Pueblos Agency (Albuquerque, New Mexico), efficiency report, May 1, 1927, with added comment by Medical Director H. J. Warner, District # 3.

5
BEYOND ASSIMILATION

When Ellen Lawrence entered the Indian Service in 1915, the BIA was holding to the coerced eradication of traditional Native American beliefs and practices and the substitution of Anglo ways for them as its philosophy of assimilation into the white world. But by 1928, when she reported for duty as assistant matron at the Albuquerque Indian School (a government boarding school), a reversal of bureau priorities and programs was underway. The inherent importance of Indian culture was increasingly recognized and the obligation to preserve and carry it forward while improving the quality of Indian life was acknowledged.

Awareness of the Pueblo cultures of New Mexico—a territory of the United States until 1912, when it was granted statehood—intensified early in the twentieth century, as artists flocked from other areas of the country to Santa Fe and Taos for inspiration. They were attracted by the dramatic physical environment, the dry, sun-drenched climate, and the rich human diversity and deep history of the place. Railroad construction from the late nineteenth century facilitated their creative odysseys. By the 1920s, Anglo artists were part of the local landscape:

> The colonies emerged about 1900 as result of a migration of artistic expatriates from what they regarded as the stifling socioeconomic atmosphere of the East. By 1920, the golden era of the movement, picturesque adobe communities of New Mexico teemed with resident artists...[who] created the prototypes for what was to become

widely accepted as western style art—mostly landscapes and people (particularly Indians or Hispanics) whose culture...[represented] the antithesis of modern industrial society...After World War I, scores of emigrés...joined the original cadre of painters.[1]

These migrant artists drew attention to the powerful appeal of Native American culture, and to its endangerment. During the 1920s, others joined them in undertaking initiatives to protect Native traditions and uphold Native rights.

Additionally, from late in the nineteenth century, anthropologists, social scientists, and archeologists documented and studied Indian history and life systematically in New Mexico. Such specialists also collected Native pottery, textiles, baskets, and other specimens of handiwork, many of which ended up in institutions far from their place of origin, raising consciousness of and concern for the indigenous legacy. In response, the School of American Archaeology was founded in Santa Fe in 1907 and, in 1909, the Museum of New Mexico as the collecting agency for the school. Devoted to excavation, research, and public education, this organization became the School of American Research in 1917 and the School for Advanced Research in 2007.[2]

In 1922, a group of anthropologists, artists, writers, musicians, and art supporters established the Pueblo Pottery Fund in Santa Fe to safeguard the heritage of Native handiwork (baskets, silverwork and jewelry, pottery, and textiles) and to carry the practice of traditional arts and crafts into the future. In 1925, this organization incorporated as the Indian Arts Fund. In 1972, when it dissolved, its collection of Native American objects was given to the School for Advanced Research.[3]

Also in 1922, the annual Southwest Indian Fair in Santa Fe was organized to maintain authenticity in Indian art and handicraft and to assure Native Americans fair compensation for their creative products:

> The Indian fair...has been held annually in conjunction with the Santa Fe Fiesta. The objects of the exhibition are to encourage and improve native arts and crafts among the Indians; to revive old arts, and to keep the arts of each tribe and pueblo as distinctive as possible; to locate and establish markets, and to secure proper prices for Indian handiwork. The management stands for the authentication of all Indian goods, and the protection of the Indian in his dealings with traders and buyers.[4]

Native-made items were displayed and sold at the fair, with prizes offered in various categories. In 1929, these categories included baskets, textiles, pottery, beadwork, paintings, Pueblo costume, miscellaneous, and school exhibits; a grand prize went to "the Pueblo which takes the most prizes in all classes."[5] An admission charge covered some of the expenses of operating the fair, with the remainder coming from donations.

In 1926, while still at the San Felipe Pueblo, Ellen Lawrence had taken great pleasure in working at the Santa Fe Indian Fair.

In the late 1910s, Native American Antonio Luhan of the Taos Pueblo in northern New Mexico met Mabel (Ganson Evans Dodge) Sterne, an emigrant east-coast Anglo. The couple married in 1923. An art patron, social reformer, and writer, Mabel Dodge Luhan was the leading personality among artists who settled in Taos, a celebrated hostess to a stunning array of creative people from elsewhere (D. H. Lawrence among them), and a champion of Native culture. She persuaded sociologist and reformer John Collier to travel to Taos in 1920 to learn first-hand about the Pueblo Indians. She and Tony Luhan guided Collier as he witnessed their ceremonies, gained an understanding of their sense of community, studied their history, and observed their living conditions.

Collier found much to criticize in the Dawes Act of 1897, by which Native communal lands were allotted as personal property to individual Indians and could consequently be sold out of tribal control. He successfully opposed the Bursum Bill, which was introduced in 1922. This bill would have allowed non-Native (Spanish and Anglo) settlers to claim Indian land on which they had squatted and could prove long-term residency, and would have transferred land disputes and Native water rights issues to state rather than federal jurisdiction. On the religious and cultural front, Collier fought against federal legislation proposed in the early 1920s to prevent Indians from performing some of their ceremonial dances.

Grasping that meaningful acculturation was impossible under BIA programs as they were then framed, Collier devoted much of the rest of his life to keeping Native culture and traditions alive and defending Indian rights.[6] In 1922, he was involved in founding the New Mexico Association on Indian Affairs, which pushed for the return to the Pueblos of land and water rights they had lost. In 1923, he established the American Indian Defense Association to protect Indian ceremonies and property. Throughout the 1920s, he was an influential steward of America's indigenous cultures. Between 1933 and 1945, when he served as the Commissioner of Indian Affairs in the progressive administration of Democratic president Franklin Delano Roosevelt, Collier had broad power to effect reform.

In 1924, Native American rights were boosted with the passage of the Indian Citizenship Act, which granted the country's indigenous people citizenship and the right to vote. Four years later, a ground-breaking report further energized the Indian reform movement. The perspective of those like Collier who were sympathetic to Native Americans' desire to live on their own cultural terms and to maintain authority over their assets was expressed in the 1928 Meriam Report, formally titled *The Problem of Indian Administration*. Requested by Secretary of the Interior Hubert Work, authorized in 1926 by the Institute for Government Research (later known as the Brookings Institution), and funded by the Rockefeller Foundation, this seminal report underscored the ineffectiveness of the BIA's overall approach to managing Indian welfare. It sparked a transformation within the agency.

The Meriam Report was a lengthy document. It touched upon a range of topics relevant to the Indian situation, which were addressed in eight sections: (1) A General Policy for Indian Affairs; (2) Health; (3) Education; (4) General Economic Conditions; (5) Family and Community Life and the Activities of Women; (6) The Migrated Indians; (7) The Legal Aspects of the Indian Problem; and (8) The Missionary Activities Among the Indians.[7] The inadequacy of government funding at its existing level was stressed throughout.

Implementation of the recommendations in the report required an about-face from earlier BIA policy:

> In the execution of this program scrupulous care must be exercised to respect the rights of the Indian. This phrase "rights of the Indian" is often used solely to apply to his property rights. Here it is used in a much broader sense to cover his rights as a human being living in a free country. Indians are entitled to unfailing courtesy and consideration… They should not be subjected to arbitrary action…The effort to substitute educational leadership for the more dictatorial methods now used in some places will necessitate more understanding of and sympathy for the Indian point of view. Leadership will recognize the good in the economic and social life of the Indians in their religion and ethics, and will seek to develop it and build on it rather than to crush out all that is Indian. The Indians have much to contribute to the dominant civilization, and the effort should be made to secure this contribution, in part because of the good it will do the Indians in stimulating a proper race pride and self respect.[8]

In adopting this radically altered outlook in the late 1920s and early 1930s, the BIA placed greater emphasis in federal Indian schools on traditional handicraft as a reflection of Native culture as well as for its potential as a source of income. Native arts and crafts classes were among Indian school offerings nation-wide by the time Ellen Lawrence's role as a field matron drew to a close.[9] The Santa Fe Indian School was evolving into a model for Native arts education, which also developed into a significant curricular focus at the Albuquerque Indian School. New possibilities appeared just when Ellen Lawrence needed them.

Moreover, the presence in Santa Fe during the 1920s of Kenneth M. Chapman—illustrator, art historian, archeologist, museum administrator, anthropologist, writer, teacher, expert in Pueblo pottery, and advocate of authenticity in the production of Indian handicrafts—both indirectly and directly benefited Ellen Lawrence as she confronted her next move within the BIA. Chapman worked for archeologist and anthropologist Edgar Lee Hewett at the Museum of New Mexico, which Hewett had convinced the New Mexico Territorial Legislature to establish in 1909.[10] He (Chapman) also took part in founding the Indian Arts Fund in the 1920s; served as a judge at the Santa Fe Indian Fair; established the Laboratory of Anthropology (incorporated in 1927) in Santa Fe and remained deeply engaged with that institution, the collections of which included Pueblo woven and embroidered items; taught at the University of New Mexico; and participated in the development of Native handicrafts programs at government Indian schools. Later, in the 1930s, he contributed to federal initiatives to promote Native craftwork. Chapman's regard for Ellen Lawrence's skills factored into her appointment in 1927 to a position at the Albuquerque Indian School.

In 1934, while John Collier was Commissioner of Indian Affairs, the Indian Reorganization Act (the Wheeler-Howard Act) ushered in the "Indian New Deal," restoring to Native Americans control of their land, mineral, and water rights and supporting their economic self-reliance. Following up on it in 1935, Congress established the Indian Arts and Crafts Board to promote the economic betterment of federally recognized American and Alaskan Indians and to develop the markets for their handcrafted products. All of this expanded upon the gains made in the 1920s. But by 1927, enough had already changed that Ellen Lawrence might reasonably hope for a situation making good use of the Native handicraft abilities she had acquired at Jemez.

On August 9, 1927, Lawrence wrote a formal letter to Commissioner of Indian Affairs Charles Burke—on Indian Field Service letterhead, typed rather than in her usual longhand—requesting a transfer "from the position of Field Matron at San Felipe to a position of teacher of Indian arts and crafts at some Indian Boarding School."[11] She added, "I have taught this work among the Indians of Jemez and San Felipe of this jurisdiction, and feel that I prefer to specialize in this rather than the other duties of the position of Field Matron." Addressed to the top-ranking administrator in the BIA by an employee considerably lower in the agency hierarchy, this straightforward statement of individual preference is remarkable. Lawrence also sent a separate package containing examples of her handiwork—a direct, personal, and concrete appeal to a powerful official who held her working life in his hands. That she was bold enough to expose her work to his scrutiny conveyed confidence in its quality.

Lawrence wrote apropos the handcrafted items in the box she sent to Washington:

> Besides the belt weaving and the embroidery like the samples, I make Navajo rugs exactly as the Indians make them, from the raw wool to the finished rug. I also do the woven beadwork. I am sorry I have none of my rugs to send you. I have made a dozen of various sizes from 18 x 30 inches to 4 x 6 ½ feet. My very first rug is in Santa Fe and I can get it if necessary. The others are lost to me. Most of them were sent east as curios.

She included return postage and requested that the commissioner send the samples back to her.

A separate typed "List of Articles in Box Sent to Commissioner of Indian Affairs" accompanied Lawrence's letter. Her selection encompassed a man's belt; patterns for women's belts; an embroidered woman's dress ("Hopi pattern. I wove the cloth on a carpet loom"); "work commenced on woman's embroidered dress. The cloth is grain bags"; men's dancing sashes (about one—only half of a sash—Lawrence commented "I wove the cloth exactly as the Hopis weave it. No loom was used"; she described the other as "Jemez pattern on cotton toweling"); a man's dancing kilt ("Jemez pattern on half of an old grain bag"); "Adaptation of Indian design. Dancing kilt pattern on a bag. I wove the cloth on a carpet loom"; a bag ("Indian embroidery on cotton toweling"); a table runner ("Indian embroidery on toweling"); and "A scrap. The Jemez Sun."

Commissioner Burke probably did not require this much evidence of Lawrence's competence nor the amount of information she offered, but the list attests to her pride in workmanship.

Lawrence's letter of August 9 is striking also for some of the references Lawrence provided in it:

> Miss Edna Groves, Supervisor of Home Economics.
> Elinor D. Gregg, Supervisor of Field Nurses and Field Matrons.
> Mr. O. S. Halseth, School of American Research, New Mexico State Museum, Santa Fe, New Mexico.
> Mr. K. M. Chapman, School of American Research, New Mexico State Museum, Santa Fe, New Mexico.
> Mr. E. H. Hammond, District Superintendent, Flagstaff, Arizona.
> Mrs. McComb, New Mexico Association of Indian Affairs, Canon Road, Santa Fe, New Mexico.

The presence of Elinor Gregg on Lawrence's list is somewhat ironic, given that Gregg's 1925 report on health conditions in the Southern Pueblos contributed to the discontinuation of the field matron position at Jemez. However, Gregg had had the opportunity to observe Lawrence in action and had, in fact, written highly in her report about Lawrence's craft skills. There is no reason to think that she would have been anything other than a positive reference for a job where handicraft abilities were central.

More significant is the fact that the names of School of American Research colleagues O. S. Halseth and Kenneth M. Chapman appear among those whom Lawrence considered able to comment on "my knowledge of the Indian arts and my ability to teach them." Her work had come to the attention of people at the forefront of promoting Native handicrafts in

New Mexico in the 1920s. She may have been posted to remote pueblos, but the circle of those involved with Indian textiles was small. Those in it were acquainted with others in the region who shared their interests. That Lawrence had earned the respect of specialists in Santa Fe attests to the authenticity of her handiwork.

Furthermore, Lawrence's School of American Research connections carried weight with the BIA administrators looking for an appropriate placement for her. Lem A. Towers, Assistant Superintendent of the Southern Pueblos Agency, submitted her request for transfer along with a letter of his own to Commissioner Burke on August 9. In his letter, he remarked that her list of references included "experts of the School of American Research. We personally have heard these people praise Mrs. Lawrence's work and express the opinion that she would make a wonderful teacher of Indian arts in a boarding school."[12] This was serious commendation.

In closing, Towers recommended that Lawrence be moved to a teaching position in an Indian boarding school, "Preferably in the southwest," and if no such position was available, that she be transferred to a boarding school as a matron (a different position than field matron) and "detailed to do this work" (that is, to teach Native handicrafts). Agency administrators were clearly taking pains to match Lawrence's uncommon skills with a job that might showcase the BIA's new-found focus on Native culture.

The only 1927 letter of recommendation to survive in Ellen Lawrence's federal personnel file is that written by Edna Groves, Supervisor of Home Economics for the Indian Field Service, who wrote Commissioner Burke on August 15:

> Mrs. Lawrence is very proficient in the old Pueblo or Hopi weaving and embroidery which the Eastern Indian Associations are very anxious to perpetuate among the Pueblo villages. It is realized that Mrs. Lawrence has not been very efficient in her present capacity and I would certainly not recommend her transfer to a matron's position

because she apparently has no housekeeping ability but in discussing the matter with Mr. Perry [Reuben Perry, Superintendent of the Albuquerque Indian School], it was thought that she might be given the position of assistant seamstress at the Albuquerque school and could at the same time take classes of girls in this native art.[13]

It's not surprising that Ellen Lawrence was perceived as having "no housekeeping ability." She had demonstrated a will as a field matron to engage in preferred activities over the standard duties of her position—she was all about the handiwork, which propensity no doubt presented some administrative challenges.

Groves suggested a salary of $900 per year for the position she proposed for Lawrence. This represented a cut from what she was making as a field matron.

As it turned out, the August 9 letters of Lawrence and Towers did not arrive at the Indian Office in Washington, which was consequently puzzled by receipt of the unexplained box of handcrafted items. This delayed the processing of Lawrence's application for transfer by some weeks. Moreover, the position of assistant seamstress at the Albuquerque Indian School was not vacant.

During the early fall, Assistant Commissioner of Indian Affairs E. B. Meritt wrote Superintendent Reuben Perry at the AIS to ask about offering Lawrence the position of seamstress or promoting the employee who then held the job of assistant seamstress to it so that Lawrence could be transferred to the vacated position.[14] On October 6, Perry wrote in response, stating that he was not convinced that Lawrence was qualified for the position of seamstress "in a school of this size" and that he was reluctant to move the current assistant seamstress (Miss Merceline McGillis) into the seamstress job because she was "only an Indian girl" (albeit "a good one").[15] Probably more important to Perry, the temporary occupant of the seamstress position ("wife of the coach") was doing an excellent job and hoped to qualify for permanent appointment. The situation was complicated. Perry asked the commissioner to "hold these matters in abeyance" until he could talk with Ellen Lawrence.

As 1927 waned, Ellen Lawrence remained in a state of suspended animation. At the beginning of November, she did not yet know whether or not she would be posted to Albuquerque.

Commissioner Burke wrote Reuben Perry on December 2, pushing him to move McGillis into the position of assistant matron, which was then vacant, if she were willing.[16] On December 7, the resistant Perry reported that McGillis did not want to transfer from the job she then held and that he did not want to force the matter because he was apprehensive lest "Miss McGillis will feel that she is transferred to make a place for a white woman and will feel it deeply."[17] (Perry may have been condescending toward Native Americans, but he was not unaware of the power of appearances.) Because Burke did not offer him an off-ramp to bringing Lawrence on at the AIS, Perry inquired whether she might be transferred to another position at the school "and be assigned to duty in the girls' building, and in connection with her work there, have an hour each day to instruct in art and to organize a class in pottery making? The Junior Red Cross is willing to pay the salary of a pottery maker." This was certainly not the resolution that Lawrence anticipated. An hour a day teaching crafts was nothing more than a sop to induce her to accept a position that would necessitate devoting most of her time to unwanted duties. Moreover, she had no experience with pottery-making. Perry seemed to have no qualms about turning her into a part-time potter to maneuver a budget-friendly arrangement. His commitment to a quality Native handicrafts curriculum was, at least at this point, secondary.

Burke acted decisively. He appointed Ellen Lawrence assistant matron at the AIS at a salary of $1020 yearly (still a reduction from what she made as a field matron, but not so drastic as that proposed by Edna Groves).[18] Neither textiles nor pottery were specified as part of the formal status change. A few days before Christmas 1927, Lawrence was directed to report for duty at the AIS; despite an outbreak of whooping cough and measles at San Felipe and some concern about managing the storage of her personal possessions, she was instructed to act as quickly as possible.[19]

Ellen Lawrence officially took up her new position as assistant matron at the AIS at the end of January 1928, with much about the scope of her position unresolved.

NOTES

1. Joseph P. Sánchez, Robert L. Spude, and Art Gómez, *New Mexico: A History* (Norman: University of Oklahoma Press, 2014, copyright 2013), 222.

2. School for Advanced Research (Santa Fe), "History of SAR," *School for Advanced Research* (website), https://sarweb.org/about/history-of-sar (accessed June 6, 2024).

3. School for Advanced Research (Santa Fe), "History of the Indian Arts Research Center," *School for Advanced Research (website),* https://sarweb.org/iarc/history (accessed June 4, 2024).

4. Southwest Indian Fair Committee, "Southwest Indian Fair, Santa Fe, New Mexico" (undated printed brochure, Kenneth M. Chapman Collection, Box 3, 89KC0.024.2, Laboratory of Anthropology Archives, Museum of Indian Arts and Culture, Santa Fe.

5. Southwest Indian Fair Committee, "Premium List, Eighth Annual Southwest Indian Fair" (1929), Kenneth M. Chapman Collection, Box 3, 89KC0.024.2, Laboratory of Anthropology Archives, Museum of Indian Arts and Culture, Santa Fe.

6. Lois Palken Rudnick, *Mabel Dodge Luhan: New Woman, New Worlds* (Albuquerque: University of New Mexico Press, 1984), 172-182.

7. As outlined in Institute for Government Research, *The Problem of Indian Administration: Summary of Findings and Recommendations. From the Report of a Survey made at the request of Honorable Hubert Work, Secretary*

of the Interior, and submitted to him February 21, 1928 (Washington, DC: Institute for Government Research, 1928), iii.

8. Ibid., 22-23.

9. Cary C. Collins, "Art Crafted in the Red Man's Image," 444.

10. Kenneth Chapman, *Kenneth Chapman's Santa Fe: Artists and Archaeologists, 1907-1931: The Memoirs of Kenneth Chapman*, edited, annotated, and introduced by Marit K. Munson (Santa Fe: A School for Advanced Research Resident Scholar Book, 2007), 51-66.

11. BIA personnel records, Ellen Lawrence, Southern Pueblos Agency (Albuquerque, New Mexico), typed letter, signed, Aug. 9, 1927, to "Commissioner of Indian Affairs," Washington, DC.

12. BIA personnel records, Assistant Superintendent Lem A. Towers, Southern Pueblos Agency (Albuquerque, New Mexico), typed letter, signed, Aug. 9, 1927, to "Commissioner of Indian Affairs," Washington, DC.

13. BIA personnel records, Supervisor of Home Economics Edna Groves, Indian Field Service (Chemawa Indian School, Salem, Oregon), autograph letter, signed, Aug. 15, 1927, to "The Commissioner of Indian Affairs," [Washington, DC].

14. BIA personnel records, Assistant Commissioner of Indian Affairs E. B. Meritt, [Washington, DC], typed letter (copy), signature stamped, Oct. 1, 1927 (date stamped), to Superintendent Reuben Perry, Albuquerque Indian School, Albuquerque, New Mexico *(hereafter cited as AIS)*.

15. BIA personnel records, Superintendent Reuben Perry, AIS, typed letter, signed, Oct. 6, 1927, to "Commissioner of Indian Affairs," Washington, DC.

16. BIA personnel records, Commissioner of Indian Affairs Charles H. Burke, [Washington, DC], typed letter (copy), signature stamped, Dec. 2, 1927 (date stamped), to Superintendent Reuben Perry, AIS.

17. BIA personnel records, Superintendent Reuben Perry, AIS, typed letter, signed, Dec. 7, 1927, to "Commissioner of Indian Affairs," Washington, DC.

18. BIA personnel records, Commissioner of Indian Affairs Charles H.

Burke, signed status change for Ellen Lawrence from field matron in the Southern Pueblos Agency to assistant matron at the AIS, undated [Dec. 1927].

19. BIA personnel records, Ellen Lawrence, [San Felipe Pueblo, Algondones, New Mexico], autograph letter, signed, Jan. 14, 1928, to Lem A. Towers, [Southern Pueblos Agency, Albuquerque, New Mexico]; BIA personnel records, Superintendent Lem A. Towers, typed letter (copy), Jan. 16, 1928, to Ellen Lawrence, San Felipe Pueblo, Algodones, New Mexico.

6
Albuquerque Indian School—A Bumpy Start

In 1928, when Ellen Lawrence assumed the duties of assistant matron at the AIS, the population of Albuquerque, New Mexico's largest city, was roughly fifty times that of the San Felipe Pueblo.[1] She had access there to urban benefits (stores, restaurants, transportation, medical services, entertainment, and cultural events) unavailable in Jemez and Algodones—all of this on top of the fact that she had reason for optimism about the direction her working life might take.

Lawrence relocated to Albuquerque just a year and a half before the Great Depression devastated the country. She was, however, not among those hit hard by this economic disaster. Millions of Americans lost their jobs, but Lawrence was spared that calamity. She remained fully employed between the stock market crash in October 1929 and her retirement from the BIA in 1936. The relatively greater security of government positions over jobs in the private sector cushioned her from the kind of life shattering loss so many others suffered. Working for the federal government was, of course, not without risk. Appropriations fluctuated from year to year, sometimes requiring the restructuring of departments and the consolidation or elimination of positions. Salaries and benefits for government workers might be pared down to compensate for reduced resources. Nevertheless, Lawrence enjoyed comparative employment security.

The AIS represented a more populated and complex ecosystem than any working environment Ellen Lawrence had yet experienced. She faced greater peer and supervisor scrutiny and had less independence there than in the smaller, more isolated California reservations and New Mexico pueblos where she had previously been posted. No doubt it took her some time to adjust to these circumstances.

But the major challenge in her move from San Felipe to the AIS early in 1928 was precipitated neither by broad economic forces, nor by a reduction in income consequent to her change of position from field matron to assistant matron, nor by the differences between the AIS and her earlier situations. Rather, it had to do with a strained relationship with her new supervisor, Reuben Perry, Superintendent of the Albuquerque Indian School. Perry alone in the long succession of Lawrence's BIA managers expressed vexation with her.

Lawrence's intense interest in Native handicrafts was lost on Perry, who approached the subject pragmatically. During his superintendency, as the Indian Service ramped up support for the preservation of indigenous cultures, the AIS did, in fact, incorporate Native arts and crafts into its curriculum. Lillie McKinney summarized:

> Mr. Perry and Mrs. Harrington [Isis L. Harrington, Principal of the AIS] were anxious to put into the school, under native teachers, weaving for Navaho girls and pottery making for Pueblo girls, a desire that came from a study of trades that might have a monetary value to the...[Indian] girls of the Southwest. The training they were receiving was for domestics in homes, for nurses, or for assistant matrons. The girls needed some training that would enable them to earn money at home. Mr. Perry took the matter up with the Indian office early in 1924, but was unable to secure funds. Next, he wrote the management of the Junior Red Cross, and was successful in securing $900 a year to pay a Navaho woman to teach blanket weaving. By 1925 fourteen looms were installed and the course has grown more and more popular for Navaho girls through the years. Shortly after the establishment of the weaving department funds were made available through the same source to pay the salary of a Pueblo woman to

instruct Pueblo girls in the making of pottery. This course, too, has become very practical for Pueblo girls. Today the government pays the salaries of these two native instructors, through Commissioner C. J. Rhoades [Rhoads]. The Indian office was more friendly toward the native crafts, for in 1931-1932 wood carving, cabinet making and Indian art were added; the next year silversmithing. Under the present commissioner of Indian affairs, John Collier, native crafts hold a high place in the curriculum.[2]

Perry ought to have been glad of the addition to his staff of an employee who might diversify the Native craft offerings of the AIS program. However, a true administrator, he took the issue on as a task to be efficiently and cost-effectively managed rather than a labor of love or personal mission.

Lawrence's nonconformity to a more or less standard BIA profile alienated Perry, who took issue with her manner as well as her mere presence. He had done his best to deflect the Indian Office in Washington from placing her at the AIS and thereby upsetting the personnel dynamics in his bailiwick. He only grudgingly found a place for her as assistant matron and had a difficult time viewing her as an asset. More than that, he made little effort to keep his opinion of her to himself. As late as August 1930, a field investigator with the New Mexico Association on Indian Affairs found cause to comment, "Mr. Perry has never appreciated her [Ellen Lawrence's] abilities and knowledge."[3] Perry would eventually recognize the good that Lawrence could do at and for the AIS, but it did not happen right away.

The AIS was one of the earliest and largest Native American boarding schools in the country. Opened in 1881, it was at first run by the Presbyterian Board of Home Missions for the federal government, coming under direct BIA control in 1886. During Ellen Lawrence's time there, the school enrolled students from the elementary grades through high school. In 1930, the enrollment was 928.[4] Reuben Perry became superintendent of the place in 1908—two decades before Lawrence arrived.[5] He remained until 1933—a total of thirty-five years—and was succeeded by Clyde M. Blair, who subscribed "to the newer views of progressive education" and believed "that children must do creative work if they are to progress."⁶ As the man in charge for a very long time, Perry was proprietary and set in his ways when Lawrence entered the scene.

3 Hawks, photographer. Aerial view of Albuquerque Indian School, 1932. Albuquerque Museum (transfer from Albuquerque Public Library). Reproduced by permission.

Various communications in her BIA personnel file make clear that Lawrence herself and those involved with her transfer to the AIS expected that teaching Pueblo weaving and embroidery would be a significant part of her work there. An October 31, 1930 memorandum in her personnel records spells this out explicitly: "In 1928 she...was taken on at the Albuquerque school for the express purpose of teaching...[Pueblo] weaving to the Pueblo, Hopi, and Zuni girls. This was intended to round out the native crafts program at this school. Navajo rug weaving and pottery making had already become part of the program."⁷

But, as emphasized in the 1930 memo, "the lack of flexibility of Civil Service regulations" and Lawrence's "lack of qualifications that could be measured by Civil Service standards" required her transfer as assistant matron, which gave her responsibilities that took precedence over craft work.[8] The Civil Service standards that ensured her fair treatment as a government employee also—in theory, at least—limited the ability to tailor the dimensions of a job to personal qualifications. The obligations of Lawrence's position prevented her from addressing the kind of work that had made the AIS seem attractive to her. By the time this memo was written, she had been "relieved of this [unsolicited responsibility] and is now supervising all of the native crafts for girls," but not before she had experienced considerable frustration and disappointment.

Reuben Perry signed off on his first performance evaluation of Ellen Lawrence on May 1, 1928, shortly after she arrived at the AIS.[9] He identified the work for which she was best qualified as "Teaching textile subjects." Based on short acquaintance with her, he gave her final summary ratings of satisfactory in all broad categories of assessment—personality, professional equipment, teaching ability, school management, discipline, and general efficiency—and also in all the more specific skills and attributes that comprised those categories, including courtesy to others, initiative, adaptability, self-control, ambition, academic preparation, spirit of cooperation, professional interest and growth, attitude toward suggestions, enthusiasm and optimism, tact, professional preparation, and executive ability. Highlighting her effort to enhance the teaching skills required by the job she thought she had taken at the AIS, he listed the title "Foundations of Educational Psychology" as a book she had read during the previous year.

The superintendent indicated in his brief narrative comment, however, that Lawrence fell short in domestic management ("Mrs. Lawrence is not apt in the duties of matron"), which officially constituted the primary responsibility of Indian school matrons and assistant matrons. The government's 1898 *Rules, Indian School Service* specified:

> 77. The matron...shall be responsible for the domestic management of the school. She shall have the care and oversight of the dormitories and...shall see that the beds are properly cared for; that the toilet of the girls is carefully made each morning; that the clothing of the pupils is kept in proper condition, and that care and attention are given the sick pupils. 78. The matron shall see that the work in the kitchen, laundry, sewing room, dining room, dairy, and other departments of domestic economy is properly performed.[10]

It had been necessary for Lawrence to take the assistant matron position to maintain her employment with the BIA. Perry's literal interpretation of what that meant—despite the intent of the administration in Washington to more closely align her job with her unique talents —prevented a transition away from domestic duties. The superintendent pushed back against interference from on high, careful to give the appearance of following directives even while resisting them.

The narrative comment in Perry's May 1928 evaluation underscores the fact that Lawrence had not yet been allowed to teach Native handicrafts: "Mrs. Lawrence...is interested in teaching lace work, carpet weaving, etc. We intend having her bring her loom to the school and make some rag carpets." This statement must have seemed to Lawrence like a carrot dangled in front of her. Small wonder, then, that subsequent reviews document her unhappiness with her job as Perry defined it.

Between Perry's first evaluation of Lawrence and his second and markedly more critical one six months later, the possibility of Lawrence's teaching pottery was again raised. In early October 1928, Assistant BIA Commissioner E. B. Meritt directed Burton L. Smith, Superintendent of the Santa Fe Indian School, to write Reuben Perry for information "relative to the advisability of considering Mrs. Lawrence for the position of instructor of pottery-making at your school."[11] Lawrence had no qualifications to teach pottery. Nevertheless, it was something of a compliment that she was under consideration for transfer to a school that would in a few years be at the forefront of Native handicraft education. The idea that she might transfer to Santa Fe would surface again in 1930.

Ellen Lawrence's November 1928 personnel evaluation suggested growing disengagement from her work. Two of the satisfactory ratings Perry had earlier given her in broad performance categories—personality and school management—had slipped to unsatisfactory, as had three of the more specific component qualities—adaptability, interest in work, and executive ability.[12] Moreover, Perry's narrative comment was caustic: "Mrs. Lawrence is not suited to the duties of matron. She is peculiar in her personality and in her mental attitude. It is understood that she gets along well with old Indians in teaching them lace work, weaving, etc." The phrasing of this last sentence suggests that Perry had still not found a way for Lawrence to teach Native handicrafts to AIS students. Unwilling to embrace the job she had been assigned, she was struggling to redefine her role in a meaningful way.

Perry's skepticism about Lawrence's fitness for work at his school was even more apparent in her April 1, 1929 efficiency record. As in November 1928, the superintendent again rated her work as unsatisfactory in personality and school management generally, and in adaptability, interest in work, and executive ability more specifically. His blistering narrative comment echoed and went beyond that in the earlier review:

> Mrs. Lawrence is not suited to the duties of matron. She is in no way a leader of young people. Neither are they attracted to her. She is peculiar in her personality and in her mental attitudes. It is understood that Mrs. Lawrence gets along well with old Indians, and has quite an influence with the Indian women on the reservation, in teaching them and working with them.[13]

Whether or not there was anything behind Perry's judgment that Lawrence was not a good mentor of young people (Lucy Yepa Lowden's later recollections cast some doubt on this), there was a real problem between Perry and Lawrence. Their discordant relationship carried potential consequences for both. In delaying Lawrence's transition to teaching Native crafts, Perry defied the Indian Office in Washington and invited administrative displeasure; in underperforming as assistant matron, Lawrence risked disciplinary action. Their stalemate needed resolving.

Fortunately for both, Merceline McGillis finally decided to transfer from the assistant seamstress position at the AIS to a school seamstress position elsewhere in the southwest, opening up Lawrence's path to the combined role of assistant seamstress and teacher of Native textile crafts. On March 19, 1929, before preparing his third evaluation of Lawrence, Reuben Perry wrote BIA Commissioner Burke about this development and to recommend that Lawrence "look after the duties of assistant seamstress which consists in supervising the mending department, and will be able to teach weaving of carpets and other crafts activities to some of the girls at the same time."[14] He concluded disingenuously, "She [Ellen Lawrence] seems quite successful with the old Indians and I shall be glad to give her a trial with the young ones"—this when his forthcoming evaluation would indicate that he had already decided she was not cut out to teach young people.

Edna Groves, Supervisor of Home Economics for the Indian Field Service, was a mediator in the relationship drama between Reuben Perry and Ellen Lawrence. She hand-wrote a mitigating addendum to Perry's harsh comment in his April 1, 1929 assessment: "It is understood that Mrs. Lawrence is to be made ass't seamstress at the Albuquerque school and allowed to do some native handicraft. It is thought that she will fit into this new job very well." Brief and to the point, this statement alleviated administrative concerns in Washington about the situation in Albuquerque long enough for it to turn around.

On April 24, 1929, the Supervisor of Indian Education completed and signed a second evaluation of Lawrence, considerably more measured in tone than Perry's of April 1—further intervention on Lawrence's behalf at a level of authority beyond Perry's. All of the unsatisfactory ratings in Lawrence's April 1 review were changed to satisfactory, with the addition of typed notes. The supervisor commented, "I suggest Mrs. Lawrence be placed in charge of a weaving room, but not of the Navajo weaver. She understands this work well. She tries hard but does not appear adapted to matron's work although she is conscientious to a fault."[15]

In his March 19, 1929 letter to Commissioner Burke, Reuben Perry recommended that as assistant seamstress Lawrence be paid what she made as assistant matron, for which position the salary was higher. She was transferring to a more limited job, but she would gain the ability to do the work she wanted to do and would maintain the level of compensation she had already reached ($1,260 per year). When motivated, the BIA could, in fact, make a round hole accommodate a square peg.

Lawrence's formal request for status change by transfer was received at the Department of the Interior office in Washington on June 1, 1929, her formal letter of appointment to her new position written on June 3.[16] She entered duty on July 1. By the spring of 1930, Ellen Lawrence finally began to hit her stride at the AIS—even Reuben Perry had to acknowledge it.

In his April 1, 1930 efficiency report on Lawrence, Perry gave her ratings of good in all categories. (The form and rating scale had changed since the previous spring—there was only one broad category, overall efficiency; there were many more specific categories; and the satisfactory/unsatisfactory scale had been replaced by one broken into excellent/good/average/fair/poor ratings.) In his narrative comment, he conceded that the disharmony of her first year at the AIS was caused by a poor match between interest and skills and work assignment: "While Mrs. Lawrence did not make a good matron, she is making a very good assistant seamstress and in addition to her regular duties, is teaching girls to operate loom and weave rugs, etc. She is now in the position for which she is best fitted and her services are satisfactory."[17] He still distinguished between her seamstress duties as her "regular duties" and her craft work. Nevertheless, he was resigned to accepting her employment at the AIS. The signature of the Supervisor of Indian Education, with a handwritten "OK" added above it, made it clear that administrative eyes were still trained on the state of affairs at the AIS.

A week later, Perry recommended a one-step promotion and pay increase for Lawrence. He explained to Commissioner Rhoads, "As Assistant Seamstress and instructor in the use of a loom and weaving, Mrs. Lawrence has been quite satisfactory and is doing a nice piece of work. She seemed out of place as assistant matron, but in her present position is at home and

Much to Learn, Much to Give

happy."[18] It was the beginning of the long-awaited fruition of skills acquired and opportunities pursued over decades—indeed, the culmination of Lawrence's BIA career.

In his annual report for the fiscal year 1929-1930, Perry took a victory lap for advancing the cause of Native handicrafts. He wrote that "an experienced Navajo instructor" had taught Navajo girls to spin, wash, and dye wool and to weave Navajo blankets, and that a Pueblo woman had taught girls to mix clay and make pottery.[19] He singled Ellen Lawrence out for special comment:

> Mrs. Lawrence, the assistant seamstress, has been successful in taking care of the repair of clothing for pupils. In addition, has taught the girls to weave carpets, rugs, and other cloth. The articles turned out are attractive, artistic, and useful. Mrs. Lawrence used a loom of her own, and a second loom has been purchased from Berea School, Kentucky, and installed.[20]

Whether Lawrence was teaching Native craft techniques or designs at this point is uncertain, but that would soon become a significant and visible part of her work, even though the BIA administration sought to employ Native Americans to teach the handicrafts of their own people as much as possible.

Just a few months after Perry prepared this evaluation, Lawrence's skills in Native textiles inspired an attempt to steal her away from the AIS to teach weaving and Pueblo embroidery at the Santa Fe Indian School. On August 5, 1930, Margaret McKittrick of the New Mexico Association on Indian Affairs wrote BIA Commissioner Rhoads in part to inquire about the possibility:

> How should we go about getting Mrs. Lawrence transferred up to the Santa Fe school?...[We] need her at the Santa Fe School to teach

the hand weaving of the cotton cloth and the pueblo embroidery. Mr. Smith [Superintendent at the SFIS] is most anxious to have her come, and as Mr. Perry has never appreciated her...I do not think he would object to the transfer being made. Mrs. Lawrence is the only person I know in or out of the service who can teach this trade...I am quite certain that Mrs. Lawrence herself would be only too delighted to make the change.[21]

By this point, of course, Lawrence's dissatisfaction with her role at the AIS had abated, and she and Perry were managing to coexist. McKittrick's recruitment scheme did not get far—lack of funding for the position she envisioned halted the attempt.

Going forward, genuine respect for Ellen Lawrence's abilities on the part of outside observers—people from beyond the AIS and the BIA—heightened agency appreciation of her Pueblo textile expertise. Her work was known to a community of Native handicraft promoters, among them Kenneth Chapman, who drew people with common interests and varied perspectives together. His knowledge and teaching skills forged connections between University of New Mexico students and those studying Native handicrafts at the federal Indian schools. And his involvement with the recently established Laboratory of Anthropology in Santa Fe, where museum collections were available for study by budding Native craftsmen and their instructors, made this resource a center for Native arts and crafts. Being part of all this validated a sense of identity that helped Lawrence transcend the discouragements of federal employment.

NOTES

1. The population of Albuquerque was 26,570 in 1930—New Mexico Economic Development Department, "New Mexico City Population, 1910-2010," https://edd.newmexico.gov/documents/new-mexico-city-population-1910-2010/ (accessed June 22, 2024).

2. McKinney, "History of the Albuquerque Indian School (Concluded)," 313-314.

3. BIA personnel records, Field Investigator Margaret McKittrick, New Mexico Association on Indian Affairs (Santa Fe, New Mexico), typed letter, signed, Aug. 5, 1930, to Commissioner of Indian Affairs Charles J. Rhoads, Washington, DC.

4. United States, Department of the Interior, Bureau of Indian Affairs, Commissioner of Indian Affairs, "Schools—location, enrollment, attendance [statistical tables]," *Annual Report of the Commissioner of Indian Affairs to the Secretary of the Interior for the Fiscal Year Ended June 30, 1930* (Washington: Government Printing Office, 1930), 58.

5. McKinney, "History of the Albuquerque Indian School (Continued) [Part 2]," *New Mexico Historical Review*, Vol. 20, No. 3 (July 1945), 207-208.

6. McKinney, "History of the Albuquerque Indian School (Concluded)," 325-327.

7. BIA personnel records, "Memorandum Regarding the Transfer of Mrs. Lawrence from Albuquerque to Santa Fe," typed memorandum (copy), Oct. 31, 1930.

8. Ibid.

9. BIA personnel records, Superintendent Reuben Perry, AIS (Albuquerque, New Mexico), efficiency record, May 1, 1928.

10. United States, Department of the Interior, Office of Indian Affairs, *Rules, Indian School Service* (Washington: Government Printing Office, 1898), 12-13.

11. BIA personnel records, Assistant Commissioner of Indian Affairs E. B. Meritt, [Washington, DC], typed letter (copy), signature stamped, Oct. 5, 1928 (date stamped), to Superintendent Burton L. Smith, Santa Fe Indian School, Santa Fe, New Mexico.

12. BIA personnel records, Superintendent Reuben Perry, AIS (Albuquerque, New Mexico), efficiency record, Nov. 1, 1928.

13. BIA personnel records, Superintendent Reuben Perry, AIS (Albuquerque, New Mexico), efficiency record, Apr. 1, 1929.

14. BIA personnel records, Superintendent Reuben Perry, AIS (Albuquerque, New Mexico), typed letter (copy), Mar. 19, 1929, to "Commissioner of Indian Affairs," Washington, DC.

15. BIA personnel records, Supervisor of Indian Education [signature undeciphered; identity undiscovered], [Washington, DC?], Apr. 24, 1929.

16. BIA personnel records, Commissioner of Indian Affairs Charles H. Burke, signed status change for Ellen Lawrence from assistant matron at the AIS to assistant seamstress at the AIS, June 1, 1929 (date stamped); BIA personnel records, Acting Chief, U.S. Department of the Interior, Division of Appointments, Mails and Files J. Atwood Maulding, Washington, DC, typed letter (copy), signature stamped, June 3, 1929, to Ellen Lawrence, [AIS].

17. BIA personnel records, Superintendent Reuben Perry, AIS (Albuquerque, New Mexico), efficiency record, Apr. 1, 1930.

18. BIA personnel records, Superintendent Reuben Perry, AIS (Albuquerque, New Mexico), typed letter, signed, Apr. 8, 1930, to "Commissioner of Indian Affairs," Washington, DC.

19. Superintendent Reuben Perry, AIS, annual report for the AIS, 1929–1930, United States, Department of the Interior, Bureau of Indian Affairs, Records, 1793–1999, Record Group 75, Superintendents' Annual Narrative and Statistical Reports, 1910–1935, microfilm, frame 958, National Archives, Denver.

20. Ibid., frames 958-959.

21. BIA personnel records, Field Investigator Margaret McKittrick, New Mexico Association on Indian Affairs (Santa Fe, New Mexico), typed letter, signed, Aug. 5, 1930, to Commissioner of Indian Affairs Charles J. Rhoads, Washington, DC.

7
Teacher of Pueblo Textile Arts

When Ellen Lawrence finally assumed teaching responsibilities at the AIS, avocation and vocation coalesced for her, unifying her personal and working identities. She acknowledged this convergence in a form she filled out to support a one-step increase in her salary in 1935. Responding to the question "What are your favorite recreations or hobbies?" she wrote, "The work I am now teaching—Pueblo weaving and embroidery."[1]

During her first year at the AIS, she had been an outsider with a shaky foothold. As her position evolved to match her sense of who she was, however, her job satisfaction increased and she became a part of the school community. Her enlarging role was reflected in consecutive issues of *The Pow-Wow*, the AIS yearbook.

Lawrence's appearance in *The Pow-Wow* for 1929—the third annual issue—was limited to the inclusion of her circa 1915 BIA personnel file photograph on the page headed "Student Advisors" and the listing of her name and position—assistant matron—in the roster of employees.[2] (Della Fisher, Margaret M. English, and Carrie G. Miller were matrons; Isadora Lucero was the other assistant matron.)

By the time the next issue was published, Lawrence was more visible in the fabric of school life. The Native Arts and Crafts Department pages in the 1930 *Pow-Wow* included a half-page photograph showing her standing behind a horizontal loom next to which was seated a Native American student. A spinning wheel sat on each side of the loom, and multiple embroidered items (presumably on hand-woven cloth) were displayed on a wall in the background and on the loom.[3] Although hardly candid, the photograph is informative—it confirms that the type of equipment Lawrence used was European-style rather than Native.[4] It also provides a glimpse of the variety of Pueblo embroidery designs with which she and her students worked. Her expertise in Pueblo textile production rested on mastery of traditional designs and stitches more than strict adherence to Native processes.

Lawrence's personnel file photograph appears again on the Home Economics faculty page of *The Pow-Wow* for 1930, and she is listed as assistant seamstress in the roster of employees (Julia E. Jones was the seamstress).[5] She also shows up in this issue in a photograph captioned "Domestic Art Class."[6]

Ellen Lawrence was featured prominently in *The Pow-Wow* for 1931. She was now a member of the Home Economics Department (Principal, Mrs. Almira Franchville) and a faculty member of the E. M. G. Club, organized in 1929 in honor of Edna Groves, Supervisor of Home Economics in the BIA.[7] Under "Club and Department Activities," she was welcomed with two other new teachers to the department.[8] The loom photograph used in *The Pow-Wow* for the previous year was run again in 1931 under the heading "Pueblo Weaving and Embroidery," with Lawrence identified as instructor and Dorothy Mahkewa and Rose Pavatea as assistants. A note specified that "Pueblo boys studying Art in U. N. M. assist with designs and weaves" (this as part of the Native arts and crafts collaboration between the University of New Mexico and the federal Indian schools, managed by Kenneth Chapman).[9]

The list of names of AIS students enrolled in Indian art courses at the University of New Mexico included Lucy Yepa, the young Pueblo artist-in-training who had first met Ellen Lawrence at Jemez.[10]

The text beneath the loom photograph in the 1931 yearbook presents Lawrence's classroom as a sanctuary for Pueblo cultural preservation: "Here the ancient weaving and embroidery of the Pueblos is carried on. Pueblo girls who wish may learn the half-forgotten weaving of their grandmothers, carrying back to their homes, not only the patterns and articles made, but the spirit of their ancient craft"—an ambitious objective to set for an Anglo instructor.

That Lawrence's education in Native handicrafts was ongoing is suggested by the closing sentence on this page—"Basketry will be added to this department as soon as possible."

The 1931 *Pow-Wow* also contains a page devoted entirely to Ellen Lawrence. Printed beneath her file head shot are two paragraphs emphasizing her role in transmitting authentic Pueblo designs to Pueblo students and, through them, back to the pueblos from which they originated:

> Mrs. Ellen Lawrence heads the department of Pueblo Weaving, Embroidery, and Basketry. An excellent weaver and lace-maker to begin with, Mrs. Lawrence readily learned the native weaving and embroidery of the Pueblos in her years among them.

> Each girl in this department will take home with her a sampler covered with true designs. These designs are to be used by the girls and their mothers and grandmothers in the making of garments, ceremonial dress and on other things for which decoration is desired.[11]

There is no mention here of the potential commercial value of embroidered articles. BIA administrators had seemingly come to understand that Pueblo weaving and embroidery did not have the marketability of some other Native handicrafts—Navajo blankets and Pueblo pottery, for example.

In any event, Ellen Lawrence's stock had clearly risen since her arrival at the AIS in 1928.

Ellen Lawrence standing by loom at Albuquerque Indian School. *The Pow-Wow, 1931. The Fifth Annual* (Albuquerque Indian School, 1931).

Lawrence's role as an instructor in Native handicrafts had taken on its full dimensions by the 1931–1932 school year. She was now able to teach what she loved as she had hoped to do. As noted in *The Pow-Wow* for that year, there were thirty-two students in her Pueblo embroidery classes—the second largest enrollment of the five AIS Indian Arts and Crafts courses (pottery making, weaving, silversmithing, pueblo embroidery, and Indian art).[12] Students at the school felt she had something to teach them.

Simultaneously, her personnel records reflect a major administrative shift in attitude toward her skills and her value as a teacher. In his April 1,

1931 efficiency report on Lawrence, Superintendent Reuben Perry rated her as average in three categories under the heading "Personal"—courtesy, personal appearance, and refinement of taste; good in seven—adaptability, consideration for others, cooperation, dependability, initiative, tact, and use of English; and excellent in three—ability to execute, industry, and originality.[13] Moreover, his narrative comment contains no hint of the fault-finding so apparent in his earlier evaluations:

> Mrs. Lawrence is carried on the payroll as "Assistant Seamstress" but is really performing the duties of instructor in native crafts. She has been provided with four looms, and is teaching the girls to operate the looms and to weave rugs. In cooperation with the principal [Almira Franchville] she has planned the teaching of basketry and materials for this purpose have been ordered.

An energizing synergy between federal objectives, local initiatives, and personal talents and aims now informed Lawrence's work.

Still, her position was not yet classified as professional. She was—on paper, at least—officially an assistant seamstress. Until the end of his superintendency in 1933, Perry did not complete the "Professional" section of any of her efficiency reports, which was reserved for "teachers and advisers only." Lawrence was not fully recognized for what she did until a new superintendent took over.

A year later, the only average rating Perry assigned Lawrence was for personal appearance. She was rated as good in adaptability; consideration for others; cooperation; courtesy, manners, conduct; dependability; refinement in taste; tact; and use of English. In ability to execute, industry, initiative, and originality, Perry found her excellent. His narrative praise was, for him, effusive: "Mrs. Lawrence is carried as assistant seamstress. The title should be changed to instructor in Indian Arts and Crafts for girls. She has wonderful ability in these lines and is entitled to have her position reclassified with a larger salary."[14] The following spring, his efficiency report for her was essentially the same except for an upgrade from average to good for personal appearance.[15]

1933 was a significant year for both the BIA and the AIS. In Washington, John Collier became Commissioner of Indian Affairs, putting the advancement of Native culture and self-determination front and center at the BIA. The creation of the Committee on Indian Arts and Crafts in 1934 and the Indian Arts and Crafts Board in 1935 were expressions of his approach.[16] In Albuquerque, Superintendent Reuben Perry and Principal Isis Harrington left their positions at the AIS and were succeeded by Clyde M. Blair and Samuel H. Gilliam, respectively. Perry's departure was followed by some reduction of staff, but Ellen Lawrence—who was rapidly becoming a poster child for local implementation of federal Indian handicrafts policy—could rest relatively secure in her position.[17]

As respect for her expertise grew at the AIS, Lawrence was afforded enrichment opportunities in the broader Native arts and crafts community. In February 1933, she attended one session of the "First Navajo Rug Project Conference" at the Santa Fe Indian School. This four-day gathering brought together Native weavers, BIA administrators and personnel, museum people and other specialists, and Santa Fe traders to explore enhancing the quality of Navajo rugs. In her report on the conference, Henrietta K. Burton (Supervisor of Extension and Industry for the BIA) wrote of the major challenge faced by those seeking to raise rug-making standards:

> For two years the staff members of the Division of Extension and Industries have been planning how to actively promote the improvement of the present output of Navajo rugs on the reservations. How to go about promoting a desirable and helpful field program without funds has been a perplexing problem...The great tribe of 45,000 Navajos have a craft whose income is in normal times about $1,000,000 a year. This important craft has been permitted to deteriorate into the production of tons of inferior rugs...[18]

Often made from readily available but non-traditional and inferior materials, featuring motifs not necessarily based on genuine Navajo designs, and sold relatively cheaply, poorly made rugs proliferated. Their abundance kept prices down, affecting income from the sale of this Native American product. Simultaneously, the transactional lens through which their making was viewed by rug sellers looking for quick profit hindered Native pride in workmanship. Burton wrote, "The Indians are being denied the pleasure and the financial profit to be derived from better products."[19]

Kenneth Chapman and Jessie Nusbaum from the Laboratory of Anthropology in Santa Fe presented at the conference, as did Chester Faris, Superintendent of the Santa Fe Indian School, and Dr. Edgar Lee Hewett from the School of American Research. Attendees, including Navajo weavers who had never seen classic rugs made by their own people, explored items from the Laboratory of Anthropology collections first-hand. (Navajo rugs were used until worn out and often did not survive for many generations beyond their production.) Some vowed to work designs and techniques they had seen into their own weaving.

Ellen Lawrence attended the afternoon session of the conference on Tuesday, February 14 at the Santa Fe Museum and School of American Research. At 1:30, Edgar Lee Hewett delivered a lecture titled "Ancient Life in the American Southwest." His presentation was followed by a tour of the museum.[20]

Hewett's lecture was geared toward building contextual knowledge rather than developing specific textile skills. How Lawrence came to be enrolled in that particular session is unknown. It is unclear whether she herself hoped to expand her understanding of the Native world or whether her supervisors selected the session for her. It is possible, too, that circumstantial factors—perhaps scheduling complexities—determined the choice.

Regardless of what prompted her presence at the Tuesday afternoon session, it seems that Hewett's subject interested her. In filling out paperwork in March 1935, she listed among the books she had read during the previous six months "Early Life in the Southwest"—likely Hewett's *Ancient Life in the American Southwest*, published by Bobbs-Merrill in 1930.[21] The theme of this volume would have resonated for a BIA employee attuned to the agency's elevation of Native American history and culture.

The year after the First Navajo Rug Project Conference, BIA Commissioner Collier wrote Superintendent Blair in Albuquerque to ask for "the loan of Mrs. Ellen Lawrence" at a special home economics conference "in the Navajo Country, at the Chas. H. Burke School" in Fort Wingate, New Mexico, and promising a "special allotment of funds...to cover her expenses"[22] It is possible that Lawrence served as an instructor for the "large group of employees...attending this meeting," but that is not spelled out in Collier's letter nor in subsequent documentation of her participation in the gathering. Whether or not she shared her skills at Fort Wingate in the summer of 1934, it is apparent that Lawrence was on Collier's radar screen as a valuable employee—someone whose strengths were to be encouraged.

Clyde Blair commended Ellen Lawrence highly as a teacher of Pueblo weaving and embroidery. In an efficiency report about her dated April 1, 1934, he assigned only good and excellent ratings in all categories for assessment on the evaluation form, and gave her an overall rating of excellent for general efficiency.

More significantly, for the first time in Lawrence's career, she was judged in "Professional" as well as "Personal" categories, and in this group of qualities and skills she received nothing but excellent ratings. Her high across-the-board professional ratings documented some aptitude for teaching. The particular attributes listed under "Professional" included" "Cultural background (with particular reference to intimate and sympathetic understanding of lives of Indian children")"; "Respect for personality of children"; Responsibility for social growth of children"; Resourcefulness as a teacher"; "Skill in directing children's activities"; and "Skill in directing children's initiative."[23] Lawrence had obviously established rapport with her students. Indeed, it is hard to see the employee described in this review as the same Ellen Lawrence who had earlier caused Reuben Perry so much administrative agita.

Almira D. Franchville, who headed the AIS Home Economics Department, wrote an extremely complimentary narrative comment for Blair's report: "Mrs. Lawrence is probably better prepared for her work than any other employee in the Indian Service. She has lived in Indian villages a number of years and has, therefore, an excellent knowledge of the lives of Indian students. She is most industrious, dependable, cooperative and efficient in her teaching." Lawrence now enjoyed the good opinion of superiors, colleagues, and students alike. She had overcome many obstacles in her working life and had realized significant fulfilment through it.

Nevertheless, a letter written by Blair to Lawrence on April 2—the day after the superintendent signed his review—seems to suggest that she kept some distance from her colleagues. She had asked for and Blair had granted her permission to take her meals "elsewhere than at the employees' club."[24] Without context, it is difficult to understand her request as other than an expression of some kind of discomfort with group dynamics. However wrong he was about her capabilities, Reuben Perry likely accurately perceived her as a nonconformist, someone more accustomed to and comfortable with autonomy—perhaps even with solitude—than with organizational interaction.

Lawrence's March 4, 1935 efficiency report reflected the positivity of that of April 1, 1934. It also foreshadowed the not-too-distant close of her career with the BIA, which enforced retirement at age sixty-five. Dorothy Ellis, Associate Supervisor of Home Economics at the AIS, wrote, "Mrs. Lawrence has been very successful in developing a course in Indian embroideries. Her work is accurate and beautifully done. Mrs. Lawrence has spent all of her free time in studying at the Pueblos. No change in location is recommended but a one-step increase in salary is recommended. The service will lose an excellent employee when Mrs. Lawrence retires."[25]

Lawrence was then almost sixty-four. Having overcome multiple challenges in attaining her position, she would hold onto it for just one more year. Her pleasure in the role of teacher of Pueblo textile arts must have been tempered by the bittersweet awareness that it would not last indefinitely. And yet, ever the learner, she was still visiting pueblos to reinforce her Native embroidery skills.

Subsequent reports in Lawrence's personnel files show that she continued to discharge her work responsibilities at a level her supervisors considered up to the mark. But, as revealed in a comment by Almira Franchville in April 1935, she developed health issues sometime after her April 1934 evaluation, which to some extent impacted the efficiency documented in her March 1934 assessment.[26] Nevertheless, no concern about her ability to effectively carry out her duties was expressed.

As Lawrence's reputation grew at the AIS and among Native crafts specialists in New Mexico, the Albuquerque press drew attention to her unusual expertise. A number of newspaper pieces referring to her and her students appeared in 1934, 1935, and 1936 in the *Albuquerque Tribune* and the *Albuquerque Journal*. Identifying Lawrence among the teachers of Native handicrafts at the school, a *Journal* article published at the opening of the 1934 school year mentioned the display in an Albuquerque store window of prize-winning items hand-crafted by AIS students and "exhibited at the Indian ceremonial at Gallup."[27] A brief notice of another exhibit of student work—"silversmithing, woodworking, ornamentation, painting, Navajo weaving, pueblo embroidery and pottery making"—ran in the *Tribune* for April 23, 1935.[28] Lawrence appeared in the list of teachers of the various crafts in that write-up, too, and in subsequent newspaper announcements of other school displays.[29]

In January 1935, the *Tribune* ran a piece about Native crafts instruction at the school. Special attention was devoted to Lawrence's work:

Under Mrs. Ellen Lawrence, 30 [i.e. 20] years in the Indian service, Pueblo girls are weaving cotton cloth to be used in making dance skirts for men and dance dresses for Pueblo women. These the Indian girls embroider in the old, traditional designs. They also learn other forms of artistic needlework under Mrs. Lawrence and Miss Lucy Yepa of Jemez, her assistant.[30]

In using Anglo looms to make good-quality cloth which was then embroidered with historic Pueblo patterns, Lawrence and Yepa—apparently neither of them a purist—fused textile handicraft practices of their two cultures.

A May 1935 article in the *Albuquerque Tribune* described the construction by AIS students of a model adobe house in traditional style, for which students made Spanish colonial furniture and a variety of other handcrafted items. Lawrence's involvement with decorative appointments for the house was reported: "The plaques, wall hangings, table runners, curtains, etc. were made in the Pueblo Embroidery department under Mrs. Ellen Lawrence."[31] Lawrence's textile expertise fit hand-in-glove with other craft specialties at the AIS in this coordinated project. If she preferred independent agency, she was nevertheless capable of teamwork.

The proliferation of publicity about Native handicrafts at the AIS during the 1930s reflected the deliberate and focused execution of federal policy. Support of Lawrence's work grew directly out of the BIA's enlightened new emphasis on Native handicrafts as a means of reawakening cultural awareness and supporting cultural preservation. Additionally, the teaching of traditional handicrafts to some extent balanced out what was otherwise a strongly practical, vocation-oriented curriculum.[32] Lawrence pursued Native textile crafts for her own reasons, but her efforts contributed toward some common goals. Her success and satisfaction in her work depended on achieving a sustainable synthesis of individual and broader interests.

1936 was a banner year for press attention to Ellen Lawrence. An *Albuquerque Tribune* article about the opening of the annual student arts and crafts exhibition at the AIS in May of the year summarized Kenneth Chapman's remarks at that event. Chapman emphasized the importance of maintaining high standards in Indian handiwork and expressed his admiration for teachers who upheld them. He commended two AIS teachers in particular—"Mr. Chapman, curator of the Laboratory of Anthropology museum in Santa Fe, mentioned specifically the work of Mrs. Ellen Lawrence and of Chester Yellowhair, who teach pueblo weaving and embroidery and Navajo silverwork, respectively."[33] The attention of Native arts devotees in Santa Fe was important in establishing Ellen Lawrence's reputation as a teacher of Pueblo textile arts. By the spring of 1936, the drumroll preceding her retirement further stimulated publicity of her work.

Ellen Lawrence wearing manta of cloth she wove and embroidered. *Albuquerque Tribune* (May 30, 1936).

A highly laudatory piece about Lawrence appeared in the *Albuquerque Tribune* for May 30, 1936. Titled "She Taught Indians How to Weave," the substantial and informative article gave her extraordinary credit for having learned and taught traditional craft skills largely without BIA support. The unnamed writer described her as "a gentle little woman of 65, who has perhaps done more than any one individual to restore to the Indian a pride in his own arts."[34] The piece continued,

> Mrs. Ellen Lawrence, who revived the lost art of weaving belts in Jemez Pueblo in 1919, and who has stimulated the recovery of the art of pueblo embroidery, is herself a weaver of the "manta" and an embroiderer not to be surpassed by any of her pupils. The last maker of belts had died about ten years before Mrs. Lawrence went to Jemez.

The initial indifference of the BIA and the Jemez Pueblos alike to Lawrence's efforts was noted: "So great was the lack of interest on the part of both the government officials and the Indians themselves, that Mrs. Lawrence, believing as she did so firmly in the importance of the ancient embroidery and weaving, bought her own materials for several years, woolen yarns for the embroidery and cotton warp string to weave the cloth." There is, of course, no indication in BIA records of Lawrence's personal investment of funds in engaging the Jemez Pueblos in Native handicrafts.

According to this article, the Pueblos were won over when they saw "the traditional designs created in bold black and red and green on their ceremonial garments, and some of the pueblo members came to her to learn how to do what their ancestors had done for centuries." The writer of the piece perceived the reciprocal nature of Lawrence's relationship with the Pueblos at Jemez, observing that throughout her residence among them, she by turns drew upon Pueblo knowledge of and then taught what she had learned about "the ancient tribal art." Her mentorship of Lucy Yepa was mentioned, as was the fact that Yepa would take Lawrence's place at the AIS as teacher of Pueblo embroidery and belt weaving after the older woman retired. A photograph of Lawrence wrapped in a handsome manta of cloth she had woven and embroidered herself complemented the account.

As the end of the fiscal year and the conclusion of Lawrence's BIA career approached, her appreciative supervisors sought to find a way for her to teach beyond retirement. Because she would receive her pension from the BIA, continued employment by that agency was not possible. On March 28, 1936, Almira Franchville wrote Dr. Sophie Aberle, Superintendent of the United Pueblos Agency in Albuquerque, to see if Aberle could work something out:

> Mrs. Lawrence has not outlived her usefulness. Having worked with her for several years at the Albuquerque Boarding School and knowing her very well, personally, I feel that she still has a valuable service to render Indian Service teachers. That she is better qualified to teach pueblo weaving and embroidery than any other person (including Indians) in the United States, would be a rash statement to make, but I believe it is a true one. She is, also, an authority on colonial weaving, lace making, crocheting, knitting, and tapestry work. Mrs. Lawrence...would be a fine teacher of teachers and an excellent consultant.[35]

A month and a half later, H. C. Seymour, Superintendent of Boarding Schools in Albuquerque, appealed to Dr. Willard W. Beatty, Director of Education for the BIA: "I wonder if there is any provision in our regulations that will allow us to continue to hire Mrs. Lawrence for another year or two. She is still hale and hearty and does a remarkable piece of work with Indian embroidery. I dislike to lose her."[36] But no workaround was found. Lawrence filled out the application form for her annuity on April 13, 1936 and retired at the end of the fiscal year, in accordance with federal regulations.

Although Willard Beatty could not come up with long-term post-retirement employment for Ellen Lawrence, he managed to secure her temporary services for six weeks during the summer of 1936 as an instructor at Fort Wingate. A short piece in the *Albuquerque Tribune* noted his involvement—"Dr. W. W. Beatty, director of Indian Education has requested her to teach weaving and embroidery design at Fort Wingate this summer. Mrs. Lawrence will be there six weeks before leaving for Wichita Falls, where she plans to stay for a while."[37] The piece concluded with the declaration, "Mrs. Lawrence is responsible for the renewed interest in the Pueblo art of embroidery and in weaving."

Having decades before authored a book about bobbin lace making for the Priscilla Publishing Company, at the time of her retirement Ellen Lawrence was planning to write a book about Pueblo embroidery. The project was reported in the *Albuquerque Tribune* in September 1936: "Designs and techniques for embroidery on the ancient ceremonial mantas and the more modern ones will be authentically described and set out in a text book which Mrs. Ellen Lawrence...is engaged in writing."[38] Lawrence's key supporters in the Indian Service encouraged her in this undertaking: "At the request of Dr. W. W. Beatty, director of Indian Education, and Dr. H. C. Seymour, superintendent of Pueblo boarding schools, she will compile the volume. It will be used as a text in the Indian schools of the southwest." The writer of the piece stated that nothing on the subject had yet been written and noted the importance of embroidery to the Pueblos, given its use on "their ceremonial mantas and other religious apparel."

This *Tribune* article reaffirmed Lawrence's role as a resurrector of dying Native arts and as "perhaps the outstanding authority on Pueblo embroidery today." Her career was summarized,

> Beginning her work with the Indians at a time when tribal and racial interest in the old forms was beginning to die out, Mrs. Lawrence studied the old designs and taught young Indian students at the Jemez school first and later at the Albuquerque Indian School how to make their own ancient ceremonial designs in beautiful vegetable dyed wool on cotton cloth which she also taught them how to weave.

Earlier published in the *Tribune*, the photograph of Lawrence in a manta she had made herself was printed again with this article.

Willard Beatty and Paul L. Fickinger (Beatty's Assistant Director of Education) did what they could to use Lawrence's proposed book to extend her connection with the agency. Fickinger suggested to Sophie Aberle that although it would be against regulations to offer Lawrence any compensation after retirement to write her book, "Unofficially, if you wish to grant her leave to remain at the school on an indeterminate basis and furnish her meals and a room, I feel sure there could be no serious objection to such an arrangement."[39] But nothing came of this suggestion.

Interestingly, Lawrence's *Pueblo Embroidery* remained on the BIA's list of forthcoming titles for some years. It was enumerated in Carrie Lyford's *The Crafts of the Ojibway* (a BIA book) as slated for future publication, but eventually disappeared from the inventory.[40] Likely the appearance in 1943 of Harry P. Mera's *Pueblo Indian Embroidery*—published by the Laboratory of Anthropology in Santa Fe— took away Lawrence's incentive to complete the volume. Interestingly, in his ground-breaking book, Mera did not acknowledge or cite Lawrence; whether he even consulted her is unknown. Since he was probably aware of her work, there may be a backstory behind her absence from his book. Or perhaps the fact that Mera was a well-educated Anglo man, closely associated with multiple Native arts organizations and projects in New Mexico, and a prolific writer on Indian crafts simply trumped Lawrence's hands-on expertise. In any event, Ellen Lawrence's *Pueblo Embroidery* never appeared in print—a regrettable loss of her deep knowledge and experience.

Late in September 1936, Willard Beatty wrote Lawrence to thank her for teaching at Fort Wingate that summer. He found her presence there "helpful and in some ways even inspiring to those who had a chance to be with" her.[41] He hoped that nothing interfered with her work on her contemplated book on Pueblo embroidery and asked where she would be located so that he could visit her the next time he was in New Mexico. His warm letter forms the final document in her BIA personnel files.

When Lucy Yepa took over Ellen Lawrence's teaching duties at the AIS, the Anglo teacher passed the baton to a Native successor. Yepa left the AIS late in 1936 to get married and was followed in the position by Lupe Sando, Yepa's cousin, also from the Pueblo of Jemez.[42] In the end, the craft that Lawrence had pursued with determination was brought full circle back to those who could rightfully claim it as their cultural heritage.

NOTES

1. BIA personnel records, Ellen Lawrence, AIS, completed employment application form, Mar. 8, 1935.

2. *The Pow-Wow of Nineteen twenty-nine...*(Albuquerque: AIS, High School Department, 1929), 32, 72.

3. *The Pow-Wow of Nineteen-thirty...*(Albuquerque: AIS, High School Department, 1930), 52. The two photographs on the page were inadvertently misplaced and the captions consequently each accompany the wrong image.

4. A photograph in the 1930 *Pow-Wow*, 51, captioned "Native Arts and Crafts Weaving Department, Mary Peshlakai Gorman, Instructor," shows students weaving on a Native American upright loom.

5. Ibid., 62, 89.

6. Ibid., 63.

7. *The Pow-Wow 1931...*(Albuquerque: AIS, High School Department, 1931), [41], [42] (issue unpaged).

8. Ibid., [43].

9. Ibid., [49].

10. Ibid., [51].

11. Ibid., [52].

12. *The Pow-Wow 1932...*(Albuquerque: AIS, High School Department, 1932), [47] (issue unpaged).

13. BIA personnel records, Superintendent Reuben Perry, AIS (Albuquerque, New Mexico), efficiency report, Apr. 1, 1931.

14. BIA personnel records, Superintendent Reuben Perry, AIS (Albuquerque, New Mexico), efficiency report, Apr. 1, 1932.

15. BIA personnel records, Superintendent Reuben Perry, AIS (Albuquerque, New Mexico), efficiency report, Apr. 1, 1933.

16. Jennifer McLerran, *A New Deal for Navajo Weaving: Reform and Revival of Diné Textiles* (Tucson: University of Arizona Press, 2022), 124-126.

17. Regarding staff reduction—McKinney, "History of the Albuquerque Indian School (Concluded)," 326.

18. United States, Department of the Interior, Office of Indian Affairs, Field Service, Division of Extension and Industry, Henrietta K. Burton, "Report of the Navajo Rug Project Conference," February 13-16, 1933, Santa Fe [typescript; copy], [1], School of American Research miscellaneous records, 1913–1995, the Catherine McElvain Library & Archives, AC17:29, School for Advanced Research, Santa Fe.

19. Ibid., [1]-2.

20. United States, Department of the Interior, Office of Indian Affairs, Field Service, Division of Extension and Industry, *First Navajo Rug Project Conference. Santa Fe Indian School. Santa Fe, New Mexico, February 13, 14, 15, and 16, 1933* [program], [3].

21. BIA personnel records, Ellen Lawrence, AIS, completed employment application form, Mar. 8, 1935.

22. BIA personnel records, Commissioner of Indian Affairs John Collier, Washington, DC, typed letter, signed, Aug. 1, 1934 (date stamped), to Superintendent Clyde M. Blair, AIS, Albuquerque, New Mexico.

23. BIA personnel records, Superintendent Clyde M. Blair, AIS (Albuquerque, New Mexico), efficiency report, Apr. 1, 1934.

24. BIA personnel records, Superintendent Clyde M. Blair, AIS (Albuquerque, New Mexico), typed letter (copy), Apr. 2, 1934, to Ellen Lawrence, AIS.

25. BIA personnel records, Associate Supervisor of Home Economics Dorothy Ellis, AIS (Albuquerque, New Mexico), efficiency report, Mar. 4, 1935.

26. BIA personnel records, Head of Home Economics Almira D. Franchville, AIS (Albuquerque, New Mexico), efficiency report, Apr. 10, 1935.

27. "700 Enroll at Indian School. Special Train Brings in Students; Gallup Exhibits Shown," *Albuquerque Journal*, Sept. 12, 1934, 3.

28. "To Hold Arts and Crafts Exhibits At Indian School," *Albuquerque Tribune*, Apr. 23, 1935, 4.

29. The April 1935 exhibit was also noticed in the *Santa Fe New Mexican*—"Indian School Exhibit in Albuquerque May 2-8," *Santa Fe New Mexican*, Apr. 29, 1935, 2.

30. "Vocational School for Indians Specializes in Native Handicrafts. Pupils Learn How to Weave, Make Pottery," *Albuquerque Tribune*, Jan. 18, 1935, 9.

31. "Indians Build Modern House. Model Residence Project Is Completed at A.I.S., Others Planned," *Albuquerque Tribune*, May 17, 1935, 8.

32. "Put Stress on the Practical. Indian School High Grades Link Vocational and Academic Work," *Albuquerque Tribune*, Dec. 20, 1935, 11.

33. "Indian School Arts and Crafts Work Should Uphold Highest Standards of Indian, Mr. Chapman Tells Students," *Albuquerque Tribune*, May 11, 1936, 6.

34. "She Taught Indians How to Weave. Revived Ancient Embroidery Designs," *Albuquerque Tribune*, May 30, 1936, 2.

35. BIA personnel records, Associate Supervisor of Home Economics Almira D. Franchville, AIS (Albuquerque, New Mexico), typed letter (copy), Mar. 28, 1936, to Sophie Aberle, Superintendent of United Pueblos Agency (Albuquerque).

36. BIA personnel records, Superintendent of Boarding Schools H. C. Seymour, AIS (Albuquerque, New Mexico), typed letter, signed, May 11,

1936, to Willard W. Beatty, Director of Education, Office of Indian Affairs (Washington, DC).

37. "Mrs. Lawrence Will Teach at Wingate," *Albuquerque Tribune*, June 8, 1936, 7.

38. "To Write Book on Indian Embroidery," *Albuquerque Tribune*, Sept. 25, 1936, 9.

39. BIA personnel records, Assistant Director of Education Paul L. Fickinger, Office of Indian Affairs (Washington, DC), typed letter, signed, Aug. 7, 1936 (date stamped), to Sophie Aberle, United Pueblos Agency ([Albuquerque, New Mexico]).

40. Carrie A. Lyford, *Ojibwa Crafts (Chippewa)* ([Washington, DC]: Branch of Education, Bureau of Indian Affairs, Department of the Interior, [1942?], 4.

41. BIA personnel records, Director of Education Willard W. Beatty, [Office of Indian Affairs] ([Washington, DC]), typed letter (copy), Sept. 24, 1936 (date stamped), to Ellen Lawrence, through the United Pueblos Agency (Albuquerque, New Mexico).

42. "New Teacher Comes to AIS. Miss Lupe Sando arrives from Santa Fe to Teach Embroidery," *Albuquerque Tribune*, Dec. 1, 1936, 4.

8
After the BIA

Ellen Lawrence inherited longevity from her mother, Cassandra Ross Duke, who lived to one hundred. Lawrence, too, lived to advanced old age. She died in 1965, at ninety-four. Her retirement, which lasted twenty-nine years, was longer than her career with the BIA.

Following her departure from the AIS, Lawrence relocated to Santa Fe, where she remained until her death.[1] Her son Henry, who ran a local business in automobile sales and service, resided there. Beyond family ties, Lawrence no doubt also found that city attractive because it was a center for arts and crafts—Anglo, Spanish, and Native American—and consequently provided outlets for her talents and a community for the serious crafter she was.

Ellen and Henry Lawrence's son had children of his own.[2] As she advanced in age, Ellen Lawrence presumably enjoyed the benefits associated with proximity to family. Her obituary noted that at her death she was survived by two of her brothers, her son, five grandsons, three great-granddaughters, and "many other relatives."[3] That she was important to her descendants is suggested by the epithet carved on the grave marker she shared with her husband—"Beloved Grandparents."[4]

Lawrence enjoyed relative health and vigor until her final days: "She was active and able to get about until about a week before her death."[5] Although she had relinquished her role as teacher of Pueblo embroidery and weaving when she left the AIS, she continued to exercise her craft skills, remaining engaged with embroidery and weaving into her ninth decade. At the twentieth annual New Mexico State Fair in September 1957, when she was eighty-six, she placed in the Home Arts Show for an embroidered wall hanging listed under the category "Miscellaneous."[6] The following year, when a record number of exhibitors submitted handicraft work, she placed again for a wall hanging.[7] In 1961, at ninety, she placed for two items—an embroidered article and a rug—in the category "Miscellaneous for Women Over 65."[8]

Ellen Lawrence died on November 11, 1965, at St. Vincent Hospital in Santa Fe. Her funeral service was held two days later, on the morning of Saturday, November 13. Dr. Robert Boshen of the First Presbyterian Church of Santa Fe officiated. Her remains were transported that afternoon to Fairview Memorial Park in Albuquerque, where her husband had been laid to rest thirty-eight years earlier.

Lawrence's need to immerse herself in handiwork was internally driven, independent of the influence of her immediate environment. Adaptive and resilient, she found a way wherever she was to exercise her prized skills. The impetus from within to work her loom and ply her needle did not depend on her being in Oak Hill, Texas, specifically, or in San Jacinto, California, or in Jemez, Algodones, or Albuquerque, New Mexico. It followed her into circumstances she could not have foreseen as a girl growing up in Missouri and Texas. It provided coherence and continuity through the vicissitudes of life.

Needlework in general and embroidery in particular have often been dismissed as women's work, devoid of true artistic merit.[9] Nevertheless, Lawrence found meaning and dignity in them. She understood—perhaps intuitively—that they represent a kind of common language and currency for women from different cultures and social strata. She knew, too, from first-hand experience, that the saleable products of handicraft work provided women of limited means a measure of financial empowerment.

Indeed, there was in her dedication to these typically female endeavors a kind of subliminal feminism. Moreover, her work among Native American women raised her awareness that the practice of textile crafts expressed cultural values that transcended practical and aesthetic considerations.

There is no indication that Ellen Lawrence either felt compelled to "save" the Native Americans she encountered during her working life or that she wanted to become more like them. She accepted the cultural and social differences between herself and the Indians of California and New Mexico and simply got on with making common cause of work that mattered to and defined her.

Lawrence's intense application to needlework and weaving may have resonated as strongly with the Native Americans she taught as did whatever specific instruction she offered. For the Pueblos, their handiwork was part of an encompassing cultural framework to be preserved and passed down. Lawrence embraced Pueblo textile arts for her own reasons, but the end result of her efforts was entirely consistent with their respect for and desire to perpetuate their own traditions.

Did Lawrence's mentorship make a calculable difference in the resurgence of interest in Pueblo textile handicrafts? It is unlikely. She was, after all, only one woman who taught a limited number of women and girls for a relatively short period of time. Still, the example of her young protegée Lucy Yepa, who practiced the craft skills Lawrence had imparted and paid tribute to her Anglo teacher's influence, testifies to Lawrence's ability to inspire her Pueblo students to greater knowledge of the creative forms of their people. She may have moved only a few toward a deeper, more proactive appreciation of their heritage, but through those few in combination with others, authentic Pueblo needlework and weaving have been brought forward.

Lucy Yepa Lowden was a poet as well as an artist, and in her writing expressed gratitude for the role of women in the preservation of Native culture. Some lines of verse she wrote in memory of her own mother allow the reader to see Lawrence within what Lowden presented as a woman-driven process of Pueblo cultural transmission:

> Let us understand what it is you speak without words,
> of how it was with the Old Ones, of lasting things
> you have preserved for our people, for all creatures
> of the universe, and in all your loving gifts
> we often fail to see and say Thank You, Mother.
> Let future women be responsive to hold steadfast
> to all these traditions and culture values.
> To let them live on without fail, eternally,
> from generation to generation.
> Women of this earth, you are the Great Ones, we praise you,
> we honor you, this is your deserved glory.[10]

Lawrence made no overt claim to particular affinity with the Pueblos she instructed. She knew she was an outsider among them. It was not her intent to appropriate their culture in any way. In mastering their weaving and embroidery, she aimed specifically to enhance and share her skill set—to satisfy her own imperatives. In doing so, she worked reciprocally with the Indian women at Jemez, participating in their guardianship of their traditions. Following her own star, she tapped into a synergy that led to both her own fulfilment and the enrichment of at least some Pueblo lives in her own time and later.

NOTES

1. Census records and city directories, accessed through *Ancestry*. The 1938 Santa Fe city directory places her on Franklin Avenue (at her son's address), the 1940 federal census and the Santa Fe directory for 1960 on Agua Fria Street.

2. "Henry H. Lawrence [obituary]," *Santa Fe New Mexican*, Jan. 4, 1994, 8.

3. "Lawrence, Ellen [obituary]," *Santa Fe New Mexican*, Nov. 12, 1965, 14.

4. "Henry Harrison Lawrence," *Find a Grave*, https://www.findagrave.com/memorial/32639857/henry-harrison-lawrence (accessed July 30, 2024).

5. "Lawrence, Ellen [obituary]."

6. "Las Vegas Woman Is Grand Trophy Winner in Fair Home Arts Show," *Albuquerque Journal*, Sept. 30, 1957, 11.

7. "Home Art Show Has Record Entry List," *Albuquerque Journal*, Sept. 29, 1958, 21.

8. "Fair Home Arts Winners Listed," *Albuquerque Journal*, Sept. 17, 1961, 38.

9. Stefanie Graf, "The Feminist Revival of Embroidery," *Hyperallergic*, https://hyperallergic.com/763837/the-feminist-revival-of-embroidery/ (accessed July 29, 2024).

10. As printed in Sando, *Nee Hemish*, 189. The poem is titled "Mother, Your Spirit Lives Within Us."

Postscript

When I began researching Ellen Lawrence's life and work in 2021, I quickly grasped that much about her story was outside my wheelhouse, which consisted mainly of subjects connected with New England history and literature. What little I knew about the life, landscape, and culture of New Mexico had been acquired through brief visits with my youngest daughter in the northern part of the state. To remedy this deficiency, in 2023 I made a somewhat longer research and pleasure trip to enlarge my understanding of Ellen Lawrence's world.

From Taos, my daughter and I took a day trip to Jemez. There, I was thrilled to get my shoes dusty with the red soil of the area, and deeply affected on entering the museum at the Walatowa Visitor Center and Museum of History and Culture to find one of Lucy Yepa Lowden's little people on exhibit.

We stopped at the visitor center store after exploring the museum. I hoped to see some modern Pueblo embroidery for sale, some possible evidence that Ellen Lawrence's efforts at Jemez in the 1920s had had an enduring impact. Although abundant specimens of pottery and other objects were displayed in and on the showcases, I did not notice any needlework. My observant daughter, however, spotted several pieces of Pueblo embroidery in the corner of one display, and called me over. With delight I examined the trim for a dance blouse and skirt made of white cloth embroidered with Pueblo stitches in vibrant red, green, and black yarn. At that moment, I felt as if Ellen Lawrence had made contact with me through the intermediacy of the Pueblo woman who had embroidered the two wrist bands and the hem band.[1] I bought them, took them back to Massachusetts, had them framed, and hung them on a wall of my home.

Every time I look at them, I wonder if Lawrence's work at Jemez really, in some way, informed the making of these particular pieces. I confess to hoping that it did. I would like to think that the relationships she forged with the women of Jemez live on in some way, even if largely forgotten. But, of course, I do not, and likely cannot, know for sure.

One thing is certain, however. This striking handiwork always evokes for me the strangely beautiful landscape and the palpable isolation of Jemez, and of Lawrence's courage and self-reliance in entering into life there. Over a career that only in its final years allowed her to be who she actually felt she was, she embraced whatever each new situation brought and pushed it toward closer conformity to her aspirations. She marched to a different drummer from others who worked for the BIA, and was fully aware that she was an outsider among the Pueblos. But she stayed the course. Although anything but a simple story, her life shows clearly that ordinary people can and do lead extraordinary lives.

LPW

1. Identified as Viola Tosa on the attached tag.

Acknowledgments

I owe a lot to my late husband Michael—my biggest fan and a valued reader—for his unfailing enthusiasm for my research and writing projects, the story of Ellen Lawrence included. I wish that we could celebrate the publication of this book together.

Our daughters Anni and Lil and daughter-in-law Dale have radiated genuine interest and support throughout this project. The day Lil and I spent visiting Jemez—where Lawrence first worked in New Mexico—was truly memorable.

Much to Learn, Much to Give could not have gotten off the ground without significant advice and assistance from National Archives and Records Administration personnel in navigating the complicated system of federal records, which include significant documentation of Ellen Lawrence's years with the Bureau of Indian Affairs. Cody White—Archivist at NARA (Denver) and Subject Matter Expert for Native American Related Records (Office of Research Services)—was particularly helpful. Kayla Dawkins (NARA, St. Louis) helped me gain access to the treasure trove of Lawrence's BIA personnel records.

I visited the Laboratory of Anthropology Archives at the Museum of Indian Arts and Culture on Museum Hill in Santa Fe in 2023. Archivist Diane Bird generously shared her expertise in the MIAC collections and offered suggestions about potential avenues of research. Librarian Allison Colborne identified useful printed sources. Collections Manager Patrick

Cruz showed me embroidered textiles in the climate-controlled MIAC vault where they are stored—one of the highlights of that trip to New Mexico.

Librarians and archivists in other institutions, too, provided support of various kinds. As always, Barbara Gugluizza, Reference Supervisor at the Concord (Massachusetts) Free Public Library, cheerfully located and sent articles as I requested them. Reference and interlibrary loan staff at the Boston Athenaeum spent significant time trying to track down elusive issues of the *New Mexico Magazine* from the 1930s. Through the efforts of Maria Carrillo Colato, Special Collections Manager at the Albert K. Smiley Public Library in Redlands, California, I was able to access the manuscript record book of the Redlands Indian Association. Pamela Pfeiffer, Public Services Manager at the Margaret Clapp Library of Wellesley College (Wellesley, Massachusetts), put a copy of *The Pueblo of Jemez* by Elsie Clews Parsons into my hands.

Others who responded to my inquiries included Librarian Katherine Wolf of the Catherine McElvain Library of the School for Advanced Research in Santa Fe, Laura Elliff Cruz, SAR Indian Arts Research Center Head of Collections, and Katelyn Ziegler, Library Information Specialist at the State Historical Society of Missouri in Columbia.

I am grateful to Brandon James and Jordan Kessler of *Pitch Black Editions* in West Concord, Massachusetts for their workmanship and patience in the preparation of the illustrations for the book.

Finally, I owe a big thank you to Dr. Sandra Harbert Petrulionis, recently retired Distinguished Professor of English and American Studies at Pennsylvania State University, Altoona. At a complicated time in her life, Sandy offered to read and respond to draft chapters of this book as I completed them. She is an all-around good friend as well as a fine scholar, and I appreciate her involvement.

De corazón, gracias a todos.

Sources

[Advertisement for *The Priscilla Bobbin Lace Book*]. *The Modern Priscilla.* Vol. XXV, No. 9 (Nov. 1911): [2].

"All Pueblos Represented in 8th Grade." *Albuquerque Tribune.* Dec. 6, 1935: 8.

Ancestry (electronic database). Accessed on multiple dates beginning in 2021 for birth, marriage, and death records, census records, voter registrations, Social Security information, directory listings, and other records relating to members of the Ross, Lawrence, and related families.

Austin, Texas. Historic Preservation Office. "A Short History of the Cotton Industry in Travis County" (typescript). Prepared by Steve Sadowsky. Oct. 2018. Item #57 PAZ. Accessible via Internet search as a PDF (accessed Feb. 25, 2024).

Barkley, Mary Starr. *History of Travis County and Austin, 1839–1899.* Second edition. Austin, Texas: Steck Company, 1967, copyright 1963.

Bartlett, William. "Red Genius Recaptured. Uncle Sam Undertakes Revival of Indian Arts and Crafts." *New Mexico.* Vol. 12, No. 10 (Oct. 1934): 28-31, 44.

Barton, Jim Tom. "Decatur, TX." *Handbook of Texas Online* (published by the Texas State Historical Association). https://www.tshaonline.org/handbook/entries/decatur-tx (accessed Sept. 19, 2023).

Benson, Martha L., and Laura Lyon Redford. *Ozark Coverlets: The Shiloh Museum of Ozark History Collection.* Springdale, Arkansas: Shiloh Museum of Ozark History, 2015.

"The BIA Field Matron Program." *Indians, Insanity, and American History Blog.* http://cantonasylumforinsaneindians.com/history_blog/the-bia-field-matron-program/ (accessed Feb. 6, 2022).

"Blount County, Tennessee." *Wikipedia.* https://en.wikipedia.org/wiki/Blount_County,_Tennessee (accessed Sept. 22, 2023).

"Bobbin lace." *Britannica Online Encyclopedia.* https://www.britannica.com/art/bobbin-lace (accessed Nov. 7, 2023).

"Bobbin lace." *Wikipedia.* https://en.wikipedia.org/wiki/Bobbin_lace (accessed Oct. 11, 2023).

"A Brief History of Overshot Weaving." Article series "Overshot Weaving." *Comfortcloth.* https://comfortclothweaving.com/article/history-overshot-weaving (accessed Feb. 2, 2024).

Brown, Mabel E. "Lace Making Among the Pueblo Indians." *Red Man.* Vol. 8, No. 9 (May 1916): 307-308.

Burns, Inez E. *History of Blount County, Tennessee, from War Trail to Landing Strip, 1795–1955.* Westminster, Maryland: Heritage Books, 2011. Facsimile reprint of original 1957 edition, which was sponsored by the Mary Blount Chapter, Daughters of the American Revolution, and the Tennessee Historical Commission.

Bursey, Joseph A. "Reviving the Art of the Weavers: The White Man Helps the Indian to Bring Back the High Standards of Former Years in Rug-Making." *New Mexico.* May 1933: 22-24, 44-46.

Burton, Henrietta K. *See under United States. Department of the Interior. Office of Indian Affairs. Field Service. Division of Extension and Industry.*

Campbell, Tyrone D. *Timeless Textiles: Traditional Pueblo Arts 1840–1940.* Santa Fe: Museum of Indian Arts and Culture, 2003.

Carter, Sybil. [Remarks on lace making.] "Reports from the Field." *Proceedings of the Eighth Annual Meeting of the Lake Mohonk Conference of Friends of the Indian.* Ed. Isabel C. Barrows. Philadelphia: The Lake Mohonk Conference, 1890: 46-48.

Chabot, Maria. "Traditional Weaving Revives." *New Mexico.* July 1936: 24, 25, 45-48.

Chapman, Janet, and Karen Barrie. *Kenneth Milton Chapman: A Life Dedicated to Indian Art and Artists.* Albuquerque: University of New Mexico Press, 2008.

Chapman, Kenneth. *Kenneth Chapman's Santa Fe: Artists and Archaeologists, 1907–1931: The Memoirs of Kenneth Chapman.* Ed., annotated, and introduced by Marit K. Munson. Santa Fe: A School for Advanced Research Resident Scholar Book, 2007.

Chapman, Kenneth. Kenneth M. Chapman Collection. Laboratory of Anthropology Archives, Museum of Indian Arts and Culture (Santa Fe).

"Chapman Talks on Indian Design To the Teachers." *Santa Fe New Mexican*. Nov. 27, 1929: 2.

Collins, Cary C. "Art Crafted in the Red Man's Image: Hazel Pete, the Indian New Deal, and the Indian Arts and Crafts Program at Santa Fe Indian School, 1932–1935." *New Mexico Historical Review*. Vol. 78, No. 4 (2003): 439-470.

Cottrell, Debbie Mauldin. "Burleson, Emma Kyle." *Handbook of Texas Online* (published by the Texas State Historical Association). https://www.tshaonline.org/handbook/entries/burleson-emma-kyle (accessed Oct. 10, 2023).

Douglas, Frederic H. *Acoma Pueblo Weaving and Embroidery*. Denver Art Museum *Leaflet* 89 (December 1939; reprinted July 1967, Oct. 1974): [153]-156.

Douglas, Frederic H. *Main Types of Pueblo Woolen Textiles*. Denver Art Museum *Leaflets* 94-95 (Jan. 1940): [173]-180.

Douglas, Frederic H. *Weaving of the Keres Pueblos: Laguna, Tsia, Santa Ana, San Felipe, Santo Domingo, Cochiti; Weaving of the Tiwa Pueblos and Jemez: Isleta, Sandia, Taos, Picuris, Jemez*. Denver Art Museum *Leaflet* 91 (Dec. 1939; reprinted July 1967): [161]-164.

"Down Life Together" [newspaper listing of marriage permits issued during the week ending Sept. 12, 1896]. *Austin American-Statesman*. Sept. 13, 1896: 3.

Dozier, Deborah. "Lace Making in Southern California." *Publications by Deborah Dozier.* https://www2.palomar.edu/users/ddozier/personal_pages/publications/lace_making_in_southern_californ.htm (accessed Aug. 8, 2022).

Dozier, Deborah. "Through a Glass Darkly." *Publications by Deborah Dozier.* https://www2.palomar.edu/users/ddozier/personal_pages/publications/thru_a_glass_darkly.htm (accessed Aug. 8, 2022).

Duncan, Kate C. "American Indian Lace Making." *American Indian Art Magazine.* Vol. 5, No. 3 (Summer 1980): 28-35, 80.

"Edith Nash." *Wikipedia.* https://en.wikipedia.org/wiki/Edith_Nash (accessed May 15, 2024).

"Ellis Prairie, Missouri." *Wikipedia.* https://en.wikipedia.org/wiki/Ellis_Prairie,_Missouri (accessed Sept. 22, 2023).

"Elsie Clews Parsons." *Britannica Online Encyclopedia.* https://www.britannica.com/biography/Elsie-Clews-Parsons (accessed May 13, 2024).

"Elsie Clews Parsons." *Wikipedia.* https://en.wikipedia.org/wiki/Elsie_Clews_Parsons (accessed Oct. 11, 2023).

Eltringham, Jennifer. "'We're not as bad as we look': Girls' Education at the Albuquerque Indian School." *The Text Message* [National Archives blog]. https://text-message.blogs.archives.gov/2016/07/12/were-not-as-bad-as-we-look-girls-education-at-the-albuquerque-indian-school/ (accessed Aug. 9, 2022).

Emmerich, Lisa E. "'Civilization' and Transculturation: The Field Matron Program and Cross-Cultural Contact." *American Indian Culture and Research Journal.* Vol. 15, No. 4 (1991): 33-47.

Emmerich, Lisa E. "'Right in the Midst of My Own People': Native American Women and the Field Matron Program." *American Indian Quarterly.* Vol. 15, No. 2 (Spring 1991): 201-216.

"Fair Home Arts Winners Listed." *Albuquerque Journal.* Sept. 17, 1961: 38.

"Farmers Respond to Postmaster; Offer Produce. Lists of Those Who Have Stuff to Sell" [including H. H. Lawrence, Route 5, Box 77, Austin]. *Austin American-Statesman.* Mar. 7, 1915: 19.

Fenton, Kathleen. "Lucy Yepa Lowden's Little People." *New Mexico Magazine.* Dec. 1975: 31.

"Field Matrons." *Encyclopedia of the Great Plains.* David J. Wishart, ed. http://plainshumanities.unl.edu/encyclopedia/doc/egp.gen.013 (accessed Feb. 6, 2022).

"Filet lace." *Britannica Online Encyclopedia.* https://www.britannica.com/art/filet-lace (accessed Nov. 7, 2023).

Find A Grave. https://www.findagrave.com/ Accessed on multiple dates beginning in 2021 for information on members of the Ross, Lawrence, and related families.

[First Navajo Rug Project Conference: newspaper articles]:

"Navajo Weavers to Hold Four Day Convention Here Next Week." *Santa Fe New Mexican.* Feb. 11, 1933: 3.

"Weavers Here for Confab." *Santa Fe New Mexican.* Feb. 13, 1933: 1.

"Weavers at Laboratory." *Santa Fe New Mexican.* Feb. 14, 1933: 1.

"Weavers End Rug Conference." *Santa Fe New Mexican.* Feb. 17, 1933: 6.

"White Men Help Navajo Women at First Rug Meet." *Santa Fe New Mexican.* Mar. 3, 1933: 6.

"First Weekly Indian Market Held Saturday at Old Palace." *Santa Fe New Mexican.* July 13, 1936: 2.

Fisher, Nora, compiler and editor. *Rio Grande Textiles. A New Edition of Spanish Textile Tradition of New Mexico and Colorado.* Santa Fe: Museum of New Mexico Press, 1994.

"For Sale" [newspaper listings of deodorized white goose feathers offered for sale by Mrs. H. H. Lawrence]. *Austin American-Statesman.* May 28, 1912: 6; May 30, 1912: 7.

Fox, Nancy. *Pueblo Weaving and Textile Arts.* Museum of New Mexico Press Guidebook Number 3. Santa Fe: Museum of New Mexico Press, 1978.

Gibson, Daniel. *Pueblos of the Rio Grande: A Visitor's Guide.* Tucson: Rio Nuevo Publications, 2011.

Goetz, Kathryn R. "Sybil Carter Indian Lace Association." *MNopedia.* https://www.mnopedia.org/group/sybil-carter-*indian-lace-association* (accessed Feb. 1, 2022).

Gordon, Beverly. "Spinning Wheels, Samplers, and the *Modern Priscilla*: The Images and Paradoxes of Colonial Revival Needlework." *Winterthur Portfolio.* Vol. 33, No. 2/3 (Summer-Autumn, 1998): 163-194.

Gordon, Sarah A. *"Make It Yourself": Home Sewing, Gender, and Culture, 1890–1930.* New York: Columbia University Press, copyright 2009.

Graf, Stephanie. "The Feminist Revival of Embroidery." *Hyperallergic.* https://hyperallergic.com/763837/the-feminist-revival-of-embroidery/ (accessed July 29, 2024).

Gram, John R. *Education at the Edge of Empire: Negotiating Pueblo Identity in New Mexico's Indian Boarding Schools.* Seattle: University of Washington Press, 2015.

Gregg, Elinor D. See under United States. Department of the Interior. Bureau of Indian Affairs. United States Indian Field Service.

"The Groundhog Comes Out." *Albuquerque Journal.* Mar. 16, 1919: 16.

Harper, Kimberly. "McDonald County." *Missouri Encyclopedia*. https://missouriencyclopedia.org/places/mcdonald-county (accessed Aug. 7, 2023).

Harris, William Torrey. *Art Education: The True Industrial Education*. Second edition of an address delivered before the National Educational Association in Nashville in 1889. Syracuse, New York: C. W. Bardeen, 1897.

"Heavy Snows in Mountain Areas During February." *Albuquerque Journal*. Mar. 17, 1919: 2.

"Home Art Show Has Record Entry List." *Albuquerque Journal*. Sept. 29, 1958: 21.

Hutchinson, Elizabeth. *The Indian Craze: Primitivism, Modernism, and Transculturation in American Art, 1890–1915*. Durham: Duke University Press, 2009.

"Indian Art Exhibit Will Open Sunday." *Albuquerque Journal*. May 9, 1936: 11.

"Indian Handcraft Series" [listing of Education Division of the Office of Indian Affairs publications in print or in planning, including an entry for Ellen Lawrence's *Pueblo Embroidery*, described as "To be published"]. Lyford, Carrie A. *The Crafts of the Ojibwa (Chippewa)*. Washington: Education Division, Office of Indian Affairs, 1943.

"Indian Institute at Sherman." *The Native American. Devoted to Indian Education*. Vol. 15, No. 28 (Sept. 5, 1914): 371-379, 386-393.

"Indian Lace Makers." *California Outlook.* Vol. 17, No. 3 (July 18, 1914): 17-18.

"Indian Reorganization Act." *Wikipedia.* https://en.wikipedia.org/wiki/Indian_Reorganization_Act (accessed Feb. 22, 2022).

"Indian School Arts and Crafts Work Should Uphold Highest Standards of Indian, Mr. Chapman Tells Students." *Albuquerque Tribune.* May 11, 1936: 6.

"Indian School Exhibit in Albuquerque May 2-8." *Santa Fe New Mexican.* Apr. 29, 1935: 2.

"Indian Students' Art Exhibit This Week; Opens with Program." *Albuquerque Journal.* May 10, 1936: 7.

"Indian Students Open Sales Shop." *Albuquerque Tribune.* Mar. 3, 1936: 4.

"Indians Build Modern House. Model Residence Project Is Completed at A.I. S., Others Planned." *Albuquerque Tribune.* May 17, 1935: 8.

Institute for Government Research. *The Problem of Indian Administration: Summary of Findings and Recommendations, From the Report of a Survey made at the request of Honorable Hubert Work, Secretary of the Interior, and submitted to him February 21, 1928.* Washington: Institute for Government Research, 1928.

"Isleta Weaving, Clothing, and Tanning—Part I." *Isleta Pueblo News.* Vol. 16, No. 5 (May 2021): 20-21.

Jacobs, Margaret D. "Clara True and Female Moral Authority." *The Human Tradition in the American West.* Ed. by Benson Tong and Regan A. Lutz. Wilmington, Delaware: SR Books, 2002. 99-115.

Jacobs, Margaret D. *Engendered Encounters: Feminism and Pueblo Cultures, 1879–1934.* Lincoln: University of Nebraska Press, 1999.

Jacobs, Margaret D. "Shaping a New Way: White Women and the Movement to Promote Pueblo Indian Arts and Crafts, 1900–1935." *Journal of the Southwest.* Vol. 40, No. 2 (Summer 1998): 187-215.

Jasinski, Laurie E. "Hubbard, TX (Bowie County)." *Handbook of Texas Online.* https://www.tshaonline.org/handbook/entries/hubbard-tx-bowie-county (accessed Sept. 19, 2023).

"Jemez Historic Site. History." *New Mexico Historic Sites.* https://nmhistoricsites.org/jemez/history (accessed Jan. 14, 2024).

Kennedy, Billy. *The Scots-Irish in the Hills of Tennessee* (Londonderry: Causeway Press, 1995).

Kent, Kate Peck. *Pueblo Indian Textiles: A Living Tradition. With a Catalogue of the School of American Research Collection.* Santa Fe: School of American Research Press, 1983.

Kessler-Harris, Alice. *Out to Work: A History of Wage-Earning Women in the United States.* 20th anniversary edition. Oxford; New York: Oxford University Press, 2003.

"The Laboratory." *Santa Fe New Mexican.* Aug. 20, 1936: 4.

"Lace." *Britannica Online Encyclopedia.* https://www.britannica.com/art/lace (accessed Nov. 7, 2023).

"Lace." *Wikipedia.* https://en.wikipedia.org/wiki/Lace (accessed Oct. 11, 2023).

"Lace Making." *Renewing What They Gave Us: Blog. Native American Collections at the Minnesota Historical Society.* https://www.mnhs.org/blog/renewing/11017 (accessed Aug. 8, 2022).

"Lace Sale to Aid Indians." *Carlisle Arrow.* Vol. 8, No. 38 (May 31, 1912): 4.

Lake Mohonk Conference of Friends of the Indian: See under Carter, Sybil.

"Las Vegas Woman Is Grand Trophy Winner in Fair Home Arts Show." *Albuquerque Journal.* Sept. 30, 1957: 11.

"Lawrence" [newspaper notice of funeral services for Henry Harrison Lawrence]. *Albuquerque Journal.* Jan. 14, 1927: 6.

Lawrence, Mary Ellen Ross (Ellen Lawrence). Autograph letter, signed, Jemes (Jemez), New Mexico, July 10, 1922, to Mildred Ross (San Antonio, Texas). Author's collection.

Lawrence, Mary Ellen Ross (Ellen Lawrence). *Bobbin Lace: Designs and Instruction.* 2nd edition. Edited by Jules and Kaethe Kliot. Berkeley, California: Lacis Publications, 1989, copyright 1979. "[U]nabridged republication of the *Priscilla Bobbin Lace Book: Designs for Torchon, Cluny, Russian and Bruges Laces with Stitches and Lessons for Working* by Ellen Lawrence, published by the Priscilla Company in 1911."

Lawrence, Mary Ellen Ross (Ellen Lawrence). "Bow in Irish Crochet." *The Modern Priscilla.* Vol. XXIV, No. 2 (Apr. 1910): 53, 59.

Lentis, Marinella. *Colonized through Art: American Indian Schools and Art Education, 1889–1915.* Lincoln: University of Nebraska Press, 2017.

"Life expectancy in the US, 1900–98." https://u.demog.berkeley.edu/~andrew/1918/figure2.html (accessed Nov. 7, 2023).

Lomawaima, K. Tsianina. "Domesticity in the Federal Indian Schools: the Power of Authority Over Mind and Body." *American Ethnologist.* Vol. 20, No. 2 (May 1993): 227-240.

Lomawaima, K. Tsianina. "Estelle Reel, Superintendent of Indian Schools, 1898–1910: Politics, Curriculum, and Land." *Journal of American Indian Education.* Vol. 35, No. 3 (Spring 1996): 5-31.

Lowden, Lucy Yepa [newspaper articles]:

> Augustine, Katherine. "Pair inspired others with their art and soul." *Albuquerque Tribune.* Mar. 16, 2000: 20.

Balsamo, Dean. "Lucy Yepa Lowden gives insight into world of her 'little people.'" *Santa Fe New Mexican.* June 12, 1992: 72.

Jones, Rebecca Roybal. "SWAIA honors five for lifetime achievements." *Albuquerque Journal.* Aug. 14, 2005: 28.

Saltzstein, Katherine. "Artist Helps Preserve Her Culture." *Albuquerque Journal.* Jan. 13, 1991: 26.

Stone, Marissa. "Jemez Pueblo artist Lowden dies at 89." *Santa Fe New Mexican.* May 6, 2005: B005.

Sullivan, Craig. "Wondrous Weaving. Demonstrations will be part of the event showcasing Native American and Hispanic artists and textiles." *Albuquerque Journal.* May 24, 1998: 127.

Lyford, Carrie A. *Ojibwa Crafts (Chippewa).* [Washington, DC]: Branch of Education, Bureau of Indian Affairs, Department of the Interior, [1942?].

"Marriages" [listing of recent marriages, including one performed in Texas County, Missouri by S. L. Ross]. *St. Louis Republican.* Nov. 27, 1876: 5.

"Maryville, Tennessee." *Wikipedia.* https://en.m.wikipedia.org/wiki/Maryville,_Tennessee (accessed Sept. 22, 2023).

Mathes, Valerie Sherer, editor. *Gender, Race, and Power in the Indian Reform Movement: Revisiting the History of the WNIA.* Foreword by Albert L. Hurtado. Albuquerque: University of New Mexico Press, 2020.

Mathes, Valerie Sherer. "The Redlands Indian Association: The WNIA in Southern California." *The Women's National Indian Association: A History.* Edited by Valerie Sherer Mathes. Albuquerque: University of New Mexico Press, 2015: 192- 210.

Mathes, Valerie Sherer, editor. *The Women's National Indian Association: A History.* Albuquerque: University of New Mexico Press, 2015.

McKinney, Lillie G. "History of the Albuquerque Indian School." *New Mexico Historical Review.* Vol. 20, Nos. 2, 3, and 4 (Apr., July, and Oct. 1945): 109-138; 207-226; 310-335.

McLerran, Jennifer. *A New Deal for Navajo Weaving: Reform and Revival of Diné Textiles.* Tucson: University of Arizona Press, 2022.

Mera, H. P. *Pueblo Indian Embroidery.* New York: Dover Publications, 1995. "[U]nabridged republication of the work originally published in 1943 by the Laboratory of Anthropology, Santa Fé, New Mexico, as Volume IV of their Memoirs."

Mihesuah, Devon A. *Cultivating the Rosebuds: The Education of Women at the Cherokee Female Seminary, 1851–1909.* Urbana and Chicago: University of Illinois Press, 1993.

Missouri Historic Costume and Textile Collection. *Textiles in Time: The James Ray Coverlets.* Edited by Laurel Wilson. Columbia, Missouri: Missouri Historic Costume and Textile Collection, Department of Textile and Apparel Management, University of Missouri, 2009.

The Modern Priscilla [issues for 1910 and 1911]. Boston: Priscilla Publishing Company, 1910, 1911.

"Mrs. Lawrence Will Teach at Wingate." *Albuquerque Tribune.* June 8, 1936: 7.

Nash, Edith. "Indian Embroidery." *Indians at Work.* Vol. 3, No. 19 (May 15, 1936): 22-25.

Nash, Edith. "Pueblo Embroidery of Exquisite Design." *Gallup Independent.* Aug. 25, 1936: 14.

The Native American. Devoted to Indian Education [periodical]. [Phoenix: Phoenix Indian School], 1900–1931. (Issues for 1914 consulted.)

"Navarro County, Texas: History Overview." *Texas Genealogy Trails.* http://genealogytrails.com/tex/prairieslakes/navarro/history_overview.html (accessed Sept. 23, 2023).

"Needle lace." *Britannica Online Encyclopedia.* https://www.britannica.com/print/article/407891 (accessed Oct. 11, 2023).

"Needle lace." *Wikipedia.* https://en.wikipedia.org/wiki/Needle_lace (accessed Oct. 11, 2023).

New Mexico. Bureau of Public Health. Original certificate of death for Henry Harrison Lawrence, Jan. 1927. *FamilySearch.* https://ancestors.familysearch.org/en/LB44-C53/henry-harrison-lawrence-i-1843-1927 (accessed Aug. 4, 2022).

New Mexico Economic Development Department. "New Mexico City Population, 1910–2010." https://edd.newmexico.gov/documents/new-mexico-city-population-1910–2010/ (accessed June 22, 2024).

"New Teacher Comes to AIS. Miss Lupe Sando Arrives From Santa Fe to Teach Embroidery." *Albuquerque Tribune.* Dec. 1, 1936: 4.

[Newspaper advertisement for Bunnell Art Company (Decatur, Texas), including reference to S. L. Ross, Dallas.] *Wise County Messenger* (Decatur, Texas). Apr. 27, 1906: 5.

"Oak Hill, Austin, Texas." *Wikipedia.* https://en.wikipedia.org/wiki/Oak_Hill,_Austin,_Texas (accessed June 19, 2022).

"Oak Hill School" (Reporters: Delmar Young and Henry Lawrence) [including notice of a "splendid declamation" given by Henry Lawrence, Jr.]. *Austin American-Statesman.* Dec. 14, 1914: 6.

Obituaries:

    Duke, Cassandra Kinkaid Slaughter Ross:

        "Former Decatur Woman Dies at 100." *Wichita Daily Times* (Wichita Falls, Texas). Jan. 6, 1949: 20.

        "Services Friday for Woman 100." *Wichita Falls Record News* (Wichita Falls, Texas). Jan. 7, 1949: 4.

    Lawrence, Henry Harrison, Jr.:

        Santa Fe New Mexican. Jan. 2, 1994: 8 and Jan. 4, 1994: 8.

Lawrence, Henry Harrison III:

Find A Grave. https://www.findagrave.com/memorial/119392553/henry-harrison-lawrence (accessed Sept. 21, 2021). "Published in Amarillo Globe-News, April 8, 2003."

Lawrence, Mary Ellen Ross:

Houston Herald (Houston, Missouri). Dec. 2, 1965: 9.

Santa Fe New Mexican. Nov. 12, 1965: 14.

Parker, Julia West:

Houston Herald (Houston, Missouri). Aug. 30, 1973: 4.

Ross, Samuel Lafayette:

Wise County Messenger (Decatur, Texas). Jan. 14, 1910: 5.

Pacheco, Ana. *Pueblos of New Mexico.* Charleston, South Carolina: Arcadia Publishing, 2018.

Parsons, Elsie Clews. *The Pueblo of Jemez.* Papers of the Southwestern Expedition, Number 3. New Haven: Published by the Yale University Press for the Department of Archaeology, Phillips Academy, Andover, Massachusetts, 1925.

"Personal Paragraphs" [including notice that H. H. Lawrence of Oak Hill was in the city the previous day]. *Austin American-Statesman.* Apr. 11, 1911: 10.

Pflaum, Jacqueline S. "Helper Woman: A Biography of Elinor Delight Gregg." Doctoral thesis, Philip Y. Hahn School of Nursing, University of San Diego, 1996.

"Philleo Nash." *Wikipedia.* https://en.wikipedia.org/wiki/Philleo_Nash (accessed May 15, 2024).

The Pow-Wow (yearbook), for the years 1929, 1930, 1931, and 1932. Albuquerque: High School Department, Albuquerque Indian School, 1929–1932.

Preble, Zahrah. [Biographical sketch of Ellen Lawrence.] "Interesting Westerners." *Sunset, the Pacific Monthly.* Vol. 42, No. 5 (May 1919): 46.

"Pueblo Indians Win Fall Trophy at Southwest Fair." *Santa Fe New Mexican.* Aug. 10, 1925: 2.

"Pueblo Weaving." *Native American Netroots.* http://nativeamericannetroots.net/diary/1270 (accessed June 27, 2022).

"Put Stress on the Practical. Indian School High Grades Link Vocational and Academic Work." *Albuquerque Tribune.* Dec. 20, 1935: 11.

Real estate transfers, Henry Lawrence [newspaper listings]:

Austin American-Statesman. Dec. 14, 1890: 13.

Austin American-Statesman. Oct. 13, 1902: 3.

Austin American-Statesman. Sept. 30, 1913: 6.

Austin American: Sept. 19, 1915: 10.

Austin American-Statesman. Aug. 15, 1923: 9.

Redlands Indian Association. Manuscript minute book, 1904–1928. Albert K. Smiley Public Library, Redlands, California.

Roediger, Virginia More, with a new introduction by Fred Eggan. *Ceremonial Costumes of the Pueblo Indians. Their Evolution, Fabrication, and Significance in the Prayer Drama.* Berkeley: University of California Press, 1991 (originally published 1941).

Rudnick, Lois Palken. *Mabel Dodge Luhan: New Woman, New Worlds.* Albuquerque: University of New Mexico Press, 1984.

"S. L. Ross was in town..." [newspaper notice]. *Wise County Messenger* (Decatur, Texas). Jan. 20, 1905: 5.

Sadowsky, Steve. See under Austin, Texas. Historic Preservation Office.

Sánchez, Joseph P., Robert L. Spude, and Art Gómez. *New Mexico: A History.* Norman: University of Oklahoma Press, 2014, copyright 2013.

Sando, Joe S. *Nee Hemish: A History of Jemez Pueblo.* Foreword by Governor Paul S. Chinana. Santa Fe: Clear Light Publishing, 2008.

Schackel, Sandra K. "'The Tales Those Nurses Told!': Public Health Nurses Among the Pueblo and Navajo Indians." *New Mexico Historical Review.* Vol. 65, No. 2 (Apr. 1990): 225-249.

School for Advanced Research (Santa Fe). "History of SAR." *School for Advanced Research* (website). https://sarweb.org/about/history-of-sar (accessed June 6, 2024).

School for Advanced Research (Santa Fe). "History of the Indian Arts Research Center." *School for Advanced Research* (website). https://sarweb.org/iarc/history (accessed June 4, 2024).

School for Advanced Research (Santa Fe). *Pueblo Textiles and Embroideries* (video of public panel presentation at the New Mexico Museum of Art, September 23, 2018; moderator Brian Vallo, panelists Louie Garcia, Aric Chopito, and Isabel Gonzales). https://www.youtube.com/watch?v=kZ-3j3lJd2M (accessed June 30, July 1, 2, and 3, 2023).

School for Advanced Research (Santa Fe). *We Dance with Them: Pueblo Indian Embroidery.* https://www.sarweb.org/embroidery/default.htm (accessed Aug. 9, 2022).

Schrader, Robert Fay. *The Indian Arts & Crafts Board: An Aspect of New Deal Indian Policy.* Albuquerque: University of New Mexico Press, 1983.

"7 Stats About Working Women to Celebrate the Women's Bureau Centennial." *U.S. Department of Labor Blog.* https://blog.dol.gov/2020/06/05/7-stats-to-celebrate-the-womens-bureau-centennial (accessed Dec. 31, 2023).

"700 Enroll at Indian School. Special Train Brings in Students; Gallup Exhibits Shown." *Albuquerque Journal.* Sept. 12, 1934: 3.

"Severe Winter But No Record-Breaker, Says Weather Man." *Santa Fe New Mexican.* Mar. 27, 1919: 5.

"She Taught Indians How to Weave. Revived Ancient Embroidery Designs." *Albuquerque Tribune.* May 30, 1936: 2.

"Sherman Institute, California." *Indian Leader. Devoted to the Interests of the American Indian.* Vol. 20, No. 4 (Sept. 29, 1916): 15-16.

Sickler, Eleanor. "Lace-Making by Indian Women." *The Native American* [reprinted from *Los Angeles Times*]. Vol. 15, No. 34 (Oct. 17, 1914): 457-459.

"Silver Convention. Ex-Governor Hogg Makes a Characteristic Speech and Declares for Free Silver. Lubbock and Col. Mills. Free Silver Convention in Austin to Select Delegates to the State Convention in Fort Worth Next Month." *Galveston Daily News.* July 21, 1895: 4.

Simonsen, Jane E. *Making Home Work: Domesticity and Native American Assimilation in the American West, 1860–1919.* Chapel Hill: University of North Carolina Press, 2006.

Smith, Ralph. "The Farmer's Alliance in Texas, 1875–1900. A Revolt Against Bourbon and Bourgeois Democracy." *The Southwestern Historical Quarterly.* Vol. 48, No. 3 (Jan. 1945): 346-369.

Smyrl, Vivian Elizabeth. "Oak Hill, TX (Travis County)." *Handbook of Texas Online* (published by the Texas State Historical Association). https://www.tshaonline.org/handbook/entries/oak-hill-tx-travis-county (accessed Sept. 27, 2023).

State Historical Society of Missouri. "McDonald County." *Missouri Encyclopedia.* https://missouriencyclopedia.org/places/mcdonald-county (accessed Aug. 7, 2023).

Sterling, Cordelia *and* Edward Canfield [newspaper notices and articles]:

[Notice of wedding of son Robert B. Sterling]. *Los Angeles Times.* Nov. 26, 1905: 78.

"Pala Squaws Will Be Taught Lace Making." *Santa Ana Register.* Oct. 29, 1910: 5.

"Memphis Inventor Dead." *Commercial Appeal* (Memphis, Tennessee). Feb. 26, 1911: 11.

"Former Memphian Dead." *Commercial Appeal* (Memphis, Tennessee). Feb. 27, 1911: 1.

"Heirs to Millions 'Can't Afford Home.'" *Pomona Daily Review.* Mar. 20, 1911: 12.

"Mrs. Sterling Speaks." *San Bernardino County Sun.* Mar. 5, 1914: 6.

[Notice of party arranged by Mrs. Sterling at Pala Indian reservation.] *Los Angeles Times.* Mar. 22, 1914: 51.

"Art Program Given at Woman's Club. Mrs. E. C. Sterling of Redlands Gives Interesting Paper, Lace Display." *San Bernardino County Sun.* Feb. 20, 1915: 7.

"Mrs. Sterling Will Show Lace Exhibit. Colton Club Women to Enjoy Rare Treat at Meeting Tuesday Afternoon." *San Bernardino County Sun.* Feb. 21, 1915: 14.

"Mrs. E. C. Sterling Accepts Invitation To Attend Colton Gathering." *San Bernardino News.* Feb. 22, 1915: 2.

"Redlands Woman Dies." *Los Angeles Times.* Apr. 16, 1916: 13.

"Sign Thumb-prints." *Los Angeles Times.* Apr. 22, 1916: 17.

"Superintendents' Districts in California." "Agency and School News [column]." *Indian School Journal.* Vol. 14, No. 2 (Oct. 1913): 69.

Sybil Carter Indian Mission and Lace Industry Association. *Annual Report, 1905–1906.* Olivia M. Cutting, President. New York: The Association, 1906.

"Teaching Indians Lace Making." "In and Out of the Service [column]." *Indian School Journal.* Vol. 14, No. 8 (Apr. 1914): 382.

Texas County, Missouri. "County History." https://www.texascountymissouri.gov/county-history/ (accessed May 30, 2022).

"Texas County, Missouri." *Wikipedia*. https://en.wikipedia.org/wiki/Texas_County,_Missouri (accessed Aug. 24, 2023).

Theisen, Terri Christian. "'With a View Toward Their Civilization': Women and the Work of Indian Reform." Master's thesis, Portland State University, 1996.

Theobald, Mary Miley. "The Colonial Revival: The Past That Never Dies." *Colonial Williamsburg Journal*. Vol. 24, No. 2 (Summer 2002): 81-84.

"To Hold Arts and Crafts Exhibits At Indian School." *Albuquerque Tribune*. Apr. 23, 1935: 4.

"To Write Book on Indian Embroidery." *Albuquerque Tribune*. Sept. 25, 1936: 9.

Trennert, Robert A. "Victorian Morality and the Supervision of Indian Women Working in Phoenix, 1906-1930." *Journal of Social History*. Vol. 22, No. 1 (Autumn 1988): 113-128.

"Two Indian Workers Attract Attention. Basketry and Lace Making in the Woman's Building Is a Very Entertaining Feature of Indian Day at the Fair Grounds..." *Riverside Daily Press*. Vol. 31, No. 244 (Oct. 12, 1916): 3.

Underhill, Ruth. *Pueblo Crafts*. Indian Handcrafts—7. Lawrence, Kansas: Haskell Institute Print Shop, 1948, for the Education Division of the United States Indian Service, Department of the Interior.

United States. Department of the Interior. Bureau of Indian Affairs. Records (Record Group 75). Superintendents' Annual Narrative and Statistical Reports, 1910–1935. Albuquerque Indian School. Microfilm; National Archives, Denver.

United States. Department of the Interior. Bureau of Indian Affairs. Records (Record Group 75). Superintendents' Annual Narrative and Statistical Reports, 1910–1935. Southern Pueblo Day Schools. Microfilm; National Archives, Denver.

United States. Department of the Interior. Bureau of Indian Affairs. Records (Record Group 75). Pala Superintendency. Correspondence of the Superintendents, 1903–1921. Lace Industry, 1914–1916. Box 14, Folder 58; National Archives, Riverside.

United States. Department of the Interior. Bureau of Indian Affairs. Records (Record Group 75). Pala Superintendency. Correspondence of the Superintendents, 1903–1921. Mrs. Edla Osterberg [Lacemaking], 1914–1915. Box 18, Folder 1031; National Archives, Riverside.

United States. Department of the Interior. Bureau of Indian Affairs. Records (Record Group 75). Soboba Superintendency. Correspondence, 1907–1920. Lace Making Class, 1916–1918. Box 8, Folder 8; National Archives, Riverside.

United States. Department of the Interior. Bureau of Indian Affairs. Commissioner of Indian Affairs. "Field Matrons." *Sixty-Second Annual Report of the Commissioner of Indian Affairs to the Secretary of the Interior. 1893.* Washington: Government Printing Office, 1893. 54-57.

United States. Department of the Interior. Bureau of Indian Affairs. Commissioner of Indian Affairs. "Lace Making." *Annual Report of the*

*Commissioner of Indian Affairs to the Secretary of the Interior...*In: *Report of the Department of the Interior...1914 [1915, 1916].* Washington: Government Printing Office, 1915 [1916, 1917]. 35; 12; 33.

United States. Department of the Interior. Bureau of Indian Affairs. Commissioner of Indian Affairs. "Report of the Commissioner of Indian Affairs." *Annual Reports of the Department of the Interior for the Fiscal Year Ended June 30, 1905. Indian Affairs. Part I.* Washington: Government Printing Office, 1906. 1-155.

United States. Department of the Interior. Bureau of Indian Affairs. Commissioner of Indian Affairs. "Schools—location, enrollment, attendance [statistical tables]." *Annual Report of the Commissioner of Indian Affairs to the Secretary of the Interior for the Fiscal Year Ended June 30, 1930.* Washington: Government Printing Office, 1930. 56-61.

United States. Department of the Interior. Bureau of Indian Affairs. United States Indian Field Service. Field Nurses and Field Matrons. Records (Record Group 75). Southern Pueblo. Central Classified Files, 1907–1939. "Report on Health Activities, Southern Pueblos. Visited April 26th to May 7th, 1925." Submitted by Elinor D. Gregg, Supervisor of Field Nurses & Field Matrons. (Additional material accompanies report.) File CCF43440-1925-700-Southern Pueblo; National Archives, Washington, DC.

United States. Department of the Interior. Bureau of Indian Affairs. Personnel Records, National Archives, St. Louis. Files for Ellen Lawrence, 1909–1936.

United States. Department of the Interior. Office of Indian Affairs. *Course of Study for the Indian Schools of the United States. Industrial and Literary.* Washington: Government Printing Office, 1901. Submitted by Estelle Reel, Superintendent of Indian Schools, Office of Indian Affairs.

United States. Department of the Interior. Office of Indian Affairs. *Outline Lessons in Housekeeping, Including Cooking, Laundering, Dairying, and Nursing. For Use in Indian Schools.* Washington: Government Printing Office, 1911.

United States. Department of the Interior. Office of Indian Affairs. *Rules, Indian School Service.* Washington: Government Printing Office, 1898.

United States. Department of the Interior. Office of Indian Affairs. *Some Things That Girls Should Know How to Do, and Hence Should Learn How to Do When in School.* Washington: Government Printing Office, 1911.

United States. Department of the Interior. Office of Indian Affairs. Field Service. Division of Extension and Industry. *First Navajo Rug Project Conference. Santa Fe Indian School. Santa Fe, New Mexico, February 13, 14, 15, and 16, 1933* [program for conference, including lists of attendees, among them Ellen Lawrence]. Two copies consulted: the Laboratory of Anthropology Library, Museum of Indian Arts and Culture, Santa Fe; School of American Research miscellaneous records 1913–1995, the Catherine McElvain Library & Archives, AC17:29, School for Advanced Research, Santa Fe (the latter accompanied by the typed "Report of the Navajo Rug Project Conference" by Henrietta K. Burton and by clippings).

"Uses 50-Year-Old Weave." *Santa Fe New Mexican.* May 10, 1934: 4.

Vaillant, George C. *Indian Arts in North America. Illustrated.* New York: Harper & Brothers, 1939.

"Vocational School for Indians Specializes in Native Handicrafts. Pupils Learn How to Weave, Make Pottery." *Albuquerque Tribune.* Jan. 18, 1935: 9.

"Weather." *Albuquerque Journal.* July 10, 1922: 1.

Whitaker, Kathleen. *Southwest Textiles: Weavings of the Navajo and Pueblo.* Seattle: University of Washington Press (in association with the Southwest Museum, Los Angeles), 2002.

"White Rock Township, McDonald County, Missouri." *Wikipedia.* https://en.wikipedia.org/wiki/White_Rock_Township,_McDonald_County,_Missouri (accessed Aug. 24, 2023).

Wilson, Laurel. See under Missouri Historic Costume and Textile Collection.

Wilson, Kathleen Curtis. *Textile Art from Southern Appalachia: The Quiet Work of Women.* "Published in conjunction with the exhibition *Textile Art from Southern Appalachia: The Quiet Work of Women.* Organized and presented by the American Textile History Museum...in association with the Center for Appalachian Studies and Services...and the Kentucky Folk Art Center..." Johnson City, Tennessee: Overmountain Press, 2001.

Wood, Mary Madeline. "Marketing the Home Woman's Product." *The Modern Priscilla.* Vol. XXV, No. 7 (Sept. 1911): 48-49.

INDEX

Aberle, Sophie, 150, 152
Albuquerque Indian School, 14, 15, 17, 21, 27, 32, 85, 87, 109, 113, 114, 118-120, 123-133, 137-153, 157, 158
Albuquerque Indian School, E.M.G. Club, 138
Albuquerque Indian School, Home Economics Department, 138, 145
Albuquerque Indian School, Native Arts and Crafts Department, 137-138
American Indian Defense Association, 17, 112
Ancient Life in the American Southwest (1930): see under Hewett, Edgar Lee
Anthropologists in New Mexico, 17, 87, 91, 110, 114
Appalachian/Ozark weaving, 27-30
Archeologists in New Mexico, 110, 114
Artists in New Mexico, 16, 85-86, 109-110, 111
Assimilation of Native Americans, 16-17, 51-52, 77, 84-85, 96, 109

Balenzuela, Agnes, 66
Beatty, Willard W., 150, 151, 152
BIA: see under Bureau of Indian Affairs
Blair, Clyde M., 125, 142, 144, 145
Boshen, Robert, 158
Bureau of Indian Affairs (also referred to as BIA, Office of Indian Affairs, Indian Office, Indian Service), 16-17, 51-69, 77-101, 109-120, 123-133, 137-153
Burke, Charles H., 92, 94, 95, 97, 98, 99, 114, 116, 117, 119, 130, 131
Burke (Charles H.) School (Fort Wingate, New Mexico), 144
Burleson, Albert S., 38
Burleson, Emma K., 38-39, 41, 58
Bursum Bill, 112
Burton, Henrietta K., 142, 143

California Indians, Campo, 58, 60, 65
California Indians, Escondido, 66
California Indians, La Jolla, 65
California Indians, Malki/Morongo, 57, 58, 62, 63, 65
California Indians, Martinez, 65
California Indians, Pala, 46, 52-55, 57-63, 65, 66, 68
California Indians, Pechanga, 60, 65
California Indians, Rincon, 60, 66
California Indians, Soboba/San Jacinto, 56-58, 60, 61, 63, 65, 66, 67, 68, 158
California Indians and lacemaking, 51-69
Carter, Sybil, 53, 54
Catholics at Pueblo of Jemez, 81, 93
Cherokee, 26, 27
Christian missionary groups, 51-53, 77-78, 113
Civil Service system, 45, 57, 58, 67, 78, 127
Collier, John, 17, 111, 112, 125, 142, 144
Colonial revivalism, 43-44
Colonial weaving: see under Appalachian/Ozark weaving
Committee on Indian Arts and Crafts, 142
Confederate soldiers and veterans, 26, 38
Crane, Leo, 13, 82
Curtis, Charles, 45

Davis, Jennie, 55, 56
Dawes Act, 111
Democrats in Texas, 37-38
Dennis, Mary E., 94

Economic Depression, 1890s, 37
Economic Depression, 1929/1930s, 123
Eight Northern Pueblos Arts and Crafts Show, 86
Ellis, Dorothy, 145
Embroidery, Pueblo, 19-20, 30, 83, 85, 86-87, 89-90, 115-116, 117, 126, 132-133, 137-140, 144-152
Episcopal Board of Missions, 53

Fairview Memorial Park (Albuquerque), 100, 158
Faris, Chester, 91, 92, 93, 143
Fickinger, Paul L., 152
Field matron position and program (BIA), 66-67, 77-80, 84-85, 94-97, 101
Field nurse position and program (BIA), 79, 94-97, 101
First Navajo Rug Project Conference (1933), 142, 143
First Presbyterian Church (Santa Fe), 158
Fisher, Della, 137
Franchville, Almira D., 138, 141, 145, 146, 150
Free silver, 37-38

Gilliam, Samuel H., 142
Gregg, Elinor D., 13, 94-97, 116
Groves, Edna M., 116, 117, 118, 119, 130, 138

Hall, Harwood, 57, 58, 66, 68
Harrington, Isis, 124, 142
Heard Museum (Phoenix), 86
Hewett, Edgar Lee, 114, 143, 144
Hogg, James Stephen, 38
Hoopa Valley Agency, 67
Hopi, 18 (ill.), 90, 115, 117, 126

Indian Arts and Crafts Act, 17
Indian Arts and Crafts Board, 114, 142
Indian Arts Fund, 17, 110, 114
Indian Citizenship Act, 112
Indian New Deal, 114
Indian Reorganization Act, 17, 114
Institute for Government Research, 17, 112
Institute of American Indian Art, 85

Jones, Andrieus (Andrew) A., 92
Jones, Julia E., 138

Kopp, (Reverend) Sixtus, 92-93

Laboratory of Anthropology (Santa Fe), 15, 86, 114, 133, 143, 148, 152
Lace and lace making, 31-33, 41-43, 44-45, 51-69
Lace and lace making, by women at home, 41-42
Lace and lace making, marketing of hand-made product, 41-42, 51-55, 62, 65-66
Lace and lace making, by Native Americans, 51-69
Lake Mohonk Conference of Friends of the Indian, 53
Lawrence, D. H., 111
Lawrence, Ellen, early years/young adulthood, 25-34
Lawrence, Ellen, farm life in Oak Hill (Texas), 37-46
Lawrence, Ellen, teaching lace making in California, 51-69
Lawrence, Ellen, as field matron, Jemez and San Felipe (New Mexico), 77-101
Lawrence, Ellen, at Albuquerque Indian School, 123-133, 137-153
Lawrence, Ellen, retirement, 145-146, 148, 150-152, 157-158
Lawrence, Ellen, *Priscilla Bobbin Lace Book* (1911), 31, 44-45
Lawrence, Ellen, *Pueblo Embroidery*, 151, 152
Lawrence, Henry Harrison (husband of Ellen), 14, 16, 34, 37-39, 45, 46, 61, 79, 93-94, 97, 98-100
Lawrence, Henry Harrison (son of Ellen), 14, 40, 61, 79, 98-99, 157
Leupp, Francis, 16
Lowden, Lucy Yepa, 21, 27, 85-87, 89, 129, 138, 147, 149, 153, 159-160, 163
Lucero, Isadora, 137
Luhan, Antonio, 111
Luhan, Mabel Ganson Evans Dodge Sterne, 111

Mahkewa, Dorothy, 138
Marble, H. P., 82, 83, 87, 91, 93
Matron/assistant matron positions (BIA), 117, 127-128
McCormick, Thomas F., 58, 59, 62-63, 68, 99, 100-101
McGillis, Merceline, 118, 119, 130
McKittrick, Margaret, 132-133
Mera, Harry P., *Pueblo Indian Embroidery* (1943), 20, 152
Meriam Report/ *The Problem of Indian Administration* (1928), 17, 112-113
Meritt, E. B., 67, 118, 128
Miller, Carrie G., 137
Mission Indians (California): see under California Indians

Missouri, 25-27, 100
Missouri, Ellis Prairie, 25
Missouri, Texas County, 25, 27, 100
The Modern Priscilla: see under Priscilla Publishing Company
Morgan, Thomas Jefferson, 77-78
Museum of New Mexico, 110, 114

Nash, Edith, 89-90
Nash, Philleo, 89
Navajo blankets and rugs, 19, 115, 126, 132, 139, 142-143, 146
Needlework as an expression of feminism, 158-159
New Mexico Association on Indian Affairs, 17, 112, 125, 132
New Mexico Commission on the Status of Women, 86
New Mexico State Fair, 86, 158
Nusbaum, Jessie, 143

Odle, Loson L., 91, 93, 94, 97
Office of Indian Affairs: see under Bureau of Indian Affairs
Osterberg, Edla C., 53, 58, 59, 61

Parker, Julia West, 100
Parsons, Elsie Clews, 87-88
Parsons, Elsie Clews, *The Pueblo of Jemez* (1925), 80 (ill.), 81 (ill.), 88, 89
Pavatea, Rose, 138
Perry, Reuben, 14, 118-119, 124-133, 141-142, 145
Presbyterian Board of Home Missions, 125
Presbyterians at Pueblo of Jemez, 11, 81, 87, 93
Priscilla Publishing Company, 42, 43, 45, 151
Priscilla Publishing Company, *The Modern Priscilla*, 33, 34, 41-42, 43-45, 91
Priscilla Publishing Company, *Priscilla Bobbin Lace Book* (1911): see under Lawrence, Ellen
Progressive initiatives to benefit Native Americans, 44, 78, 112-113, 114, 125-126, 141, 147
Pueblo Embroidery: see under Lawrence, Ellen
Pueblos (New Mexico), Acoma, 20, 81, 85
Pueblos (New Mexico), Isleta, 81, 87, 98
Pueblos (New Mexico), Jemez, 11-14, 29-30, 79-96, 149, 160

Pueblos (New Mexico), Laguna, 81
Pueblos (New Mexico), Pecos, 13, 15
Pueblos (New Mexico), San Felipe, 81, 94, 97-101, 120, 123
Pueblos (New Mexico), Sandia, 81
Pueblos (New Mexico), Santa Ana, 81
Pueblos (New Mexico), Zia, 81
Pueblo Pottery Fund, 110
Pueblo weaving, 18-20, 28-30, 83, 85-87, 88-89, 90, 91, 115, 117, 126, 131, 132-133, 137-140, 144, 147, 148, 150, 151

Quinton, Amelia Stone, 52

Redlands Indian Association (RIA), 46, 52-57, 77
Reel, Estelle, 16, 51
"Report on Health Activities, Southern Pueblos" (1925): see under Gregg, Elinor D.
Rhoads, Charles J., 125, 131, 132
Riverside County Fair (California), 61, 62
Roosevelt, Franklin Delano, 17, 112
Ross family, Cassandra Kincaid Slaughter Ross Duke, 25, 27, 28, 30, 31, 157
Ross family, James Thomas Ross, 25-26
Ross family, Mahala Prigmore Ross, 25, 27
Ross family, Mildred Ross, 11, 12 (ill.), 13, 14, 27, 84
Ross family, Samuel Lafayette Ross, 25-27, 30-31, 40
Ross family, siblings of Mary Ellen Ross Lawrence, 27, 30

Salem School (Chemawa, Oregon), 61
Sando, Lupe, 153
Santa Fe Indian Market, 86
Santa Fe Indian School, 17, 85, 113, 128, 132, 142, 143
School for Advanced Research, 29, 110
School of American Archaeology, 110
School of American Research, 110, 116-117, 143
Scots-Irish, 14, 25, 26
Seamstress/assistant seamstress positions (BIA), 118, 130, 131, 132, 138, 141
Sells, Cato, 39, 51, 54, 57, 58, 60, 63, 65, 67, 68, 79

Service ("helping") jobs for women, 78
Seymour, H. C., 150, 151
Shafer, Lenore, 98
Sherman Institute, 61
Siebert, Anna, 92
Smith, Ada L., 65-66
Smith, Burton L., 128, 133
Social scientists in New Mexico, 17, 110
Southern Pueblos Agency, 13, 79, 81, 82, 91, 97, 117
Southwest Indian Fair, 110-111
Southwestern Association for Indian Arts, 86
Spanish influenza pandemic, 67
Sterling, Cordelia, 43, 45, 46, 53-59, 62-65, 68
Sybil Carter Indian Lace Association, 53, 65

Tennessee, 25-26
Tennessee, Maryville (Blount County), 25
Tenorio, Santana, 99, 100
Tewa Weaving Industry, 87
Texas, 27, 30-31, 32-34, 37-43, 45, 46
Texas, Austin, 34, 37, 38, 39-40, 42
Texas, Decatur, 30
Texas, Hill County, 30, 31
Texas, Navarro County, 30,
Texas, Oak Hill, 34, 39, 40, 41, 43, 46
Texas, San Saba County, 30
Texas, Travis County, 38, 39-40
Texas, Wise County, 30-31
Third Liberty Loan, 66
Tosa, Viola, 164 (note)
Towa (language), 13
Towers, Lem A., 117, 118

United Pueblos Agency, 150
University of New Mexico, 27, 85, 114, 133, 138

Valentine, Robert Grosvenor, 45-46
Valenzuela, Salvadora, 61, 62-63

Wadsworth, H. E., 66
Walatowa, 13
Walatowa Visitor Center and Museum of History and Culture, 163
Warner, H. J., 101
Weaving: see under Appalachian/Ozark weaving and under Pueblo weaving
Women's National Indian Association (WNIA), 52, 77
Wheeler-Howard Act: see under Indian Reorganization Act

Yellowhair, Chester, 148
Yepa, Lucy: see under Lowden, Lucy Yepa
Young, S. A. M., 97-99

Zuni, 20, 89-90, 91, 126

www.ingramcontent.com/pod-product-compliance
Lightning Source LLC
Chambersburg PA
CBHW050526170426
43201CB00013B/2101